ARISAIG AND MORAR

Arisaig and Morar

A History

DENIS RIXSON

BIRLINN

This edition published in 2011 by
Birlinn Ltd
West Newington House
10 Newington Road
Edinburgh
EH9 1QS

First published in 2002 by
Tuckwell Press, East Lothian

ISBN: 978 1 84158 978 7

British Library Cataloguing-in-Publication data
A catalogue record is available on request from the British Library

Typeset by Carnegie Publishing Ltd, Lancaster
Printed and bound in the UK by CPI

CONTENTS

LIST OF ILLUSTRATIONS

Maps

Figures

Plates

Picture credits

INTRODUCTION

This book offers a history of Arisaig and Morar – an area so typical that it was known as 'the Highlands of the Highlands'. But it is *a* history, not *the* history of the district. We are dealing with a wide area over a long period of time. Its remoteness, the absence of written records and the accidents of history mean that we have more evidence for some centuries than others. From the historian's perspective the question of what evidence *survives* prejudges the issue of what evidence to *select*.

For much of the prehistoric period little can be said apart from recording the material remains that have been uncovered. In the absence of any proper archaeological excavation we have only the barest details to help us. In the other chapters I have made no attempt to accommodate every recorded fact. Instead I have selected those areas where the evidence allows us to sketch a likeness. Sometimes, as with the Jacobites or the Clearances, I am retelling a story that has been told before. In other topics, such as Norse land-assessment or with regard to Rore Ranaldson, the material is new.

One issue which the historian has to grapple with is how we *perceive* the past and our natural environment. To a large extent this has already been set in the public consciousness by previous generations of historians. We inherit their perceptions and sometimes they can be a heavy burden to us. For, like anything human, these perceptions have themselves a history. In the eighteenth century the Rough Bounds – at the heart of which lie Arisaig and Morar – was a 'den of thieves' and 'an unmix'd nest of Popery'. Today, you could stock a library with gushing tomes about the Jacobites, but barely fill a shelf with those about social or economic conditions. In past times the Highland hills were viewed as 'horrid' or 'melancholy', the glens dark and forbidding, the houses mean and squalid. Now, the tourist literature will blandish us with images of 'bustling' fishing ports or 'tranquil' villages nestling 'neath heather-clad hills. It is not just the hills that are purple, the vocabulary alone tells a story.

It is perhaps never good for a historian to have a purpose but to the extent that I have one it is that, by retelling the story, I can inject a degree of balance and strike a note of realism. Historians must endeavour to tell the truth, the many different truths, but the mere process of selection informs our present perspective. Highland history is perpetually being hijacked to set or reinforce a current agenda.

For example any history that doesn't take the moral high ground when reviewing the Clearances immediately runs the risk of being branded revisionist. But the fact of the matter is that the communities of Arisaig and Morar have survived clearance. Why is the population now almost as high as it has ever been, albeit with a different distribution? Why is it that the indigenous families, despite a steady stream of incomers, have survived here when elsewhere they have disappeared? There are still plenty of children called Gillies, Mac-Lellan and MacEachen at the local schools.

Depopulation is partly about clearance – but it is also about economics. It is about ways of making a living – and also about changing expectations. When people are forced to leave by landlords, we talk of clearance. When people are forced to leave by economic pressure, then the issues are less clear-cut. There is no individual to take the blame but, if we are being honest, we must still face the problem. The richer economies today suck in economic migrants from marginal areas as richer economies have always done. It is not something we should be glibly moralistic about.

The survival of the indigenous population in Morar and Arisaig is partly about the failure of agriculture, but it is also about the success of fishing. Long before there was crofting there was a sea-based economy in the Highlands and Islands. If we could look past the historical dead weights of Jacobitism and Clearance, there are other histories to be written. They are often bloody, but they are not all tragic and perhaps they can provide a framework for some of the future canvases we paint.

Arisaig and Morar now consist of a number of different settlements, each making their living in a slightly different way. But, compared to some Highland areas we have relatively good communications with the outside world. There is a road, however unsatisfactory, and a railway line and employment opportunities. The area has a strategic value in the overall communications network. It is the link to

Knoydart, Skye and the Small Isles. Further growth is possible. Compared to many localities in the West it can be confident in its immediate past and hopeful for the future.

Acknowledgements

I owe a good deal to the staff of Highland Council Library Service. Studying in a remote location is difficult, and they have helped greatly. I should like to thank Norman Newton, Gail Priddice and Edwina Burridge for all their assistance and in particular Sue Skelton and Lorna Skelly for so patiently fulfilling my endless requests. I am also much indebted to Mr C. Fleet and Mr A Lloyd of the Map Library in the National Library of Scotland; and to Nicola Beech of the Map Room in the British Library.

I should like to thank Mr P Galbraith, Mr A Maclellan, Mr A Roberts, for particular items of information and Mr A Cargill for his generous advice, over many years, on matters photographic.

I am grateful to the Public Archives and Records Office of Prince Edward Island, Canada, for permission to publish the Glenaladale indenture to Donald Gilles, Accession No. 2664, Item No. 138. I also thank Arisaig WRI for permission to study the 'Arisaig Scrapbook'. I have been unable to establish the copyright owner, if any, of the Boulton Map (Plate 13). I would be glad to rectify this omission.

Note

Place-names in the Highlands and Hebrides can be spelled in a bewildering number of ways. For ease of identification I have generally followed modern Ordnance Survey spellings. Exceptions occur when I am quoting from a source and want my accompanying text to match.

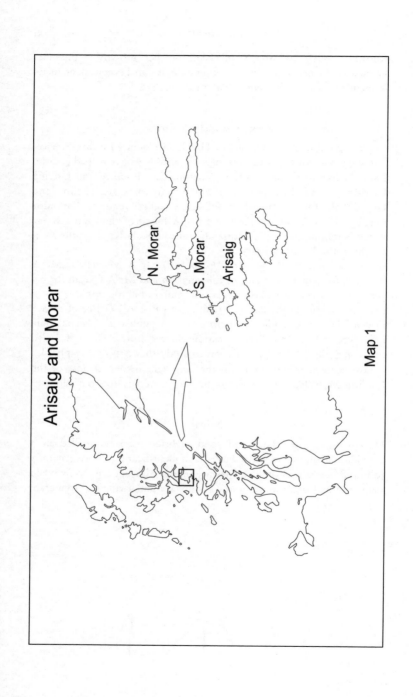

Arisaig and Morar

N. Morar

S. Morar

Arisaig

Map 1

CHAPTER I

GEOGRAPHY, GEOLOGY AND PREHISTORY

Geography and Topography

Morar and Arisaig are the names for the area between Loch Nevis on the north and Loch nan Uamh and Loch Ailort on the south (see Maps 1 and 2). The district straddles Loch Morar, and its eastern boundary is defined by the watershed towards Loch Arkaig. North Morar is easily described as the area on the north side of Loch Morar. South Morar and Arisaig are less easily distinguished in geographical terms although in an historical context they refer to separate estates. In the early mediaeval period the whole area belonged to the Macruaris and then the Clanranalds. After about 1501 North Morar was detached to become part of Glengarry's lands.

Our earliest descriptions date to around 1600 and accurately encapsulate the physical disadvantages of the area. They were probably originally penned by Timothy Pont, the father of Scottish cartography, and later copies eventually found their way into *Macfarlane's Geographical Collections*. There they survive in two versions whose close similarities indicate a common origin. The following extract refers to Arisaig and South Morar (which belonged to Clanranald), then to North Morar. There is a close correspondence between the names given here and those which appear on Robert Gordon's maps, a fact that increases the likelihood of Pont's authorship:

> Arysaig cumeth after, nixt to Muideort, it is no corne countrey but for pasture and fishes, it hath a Church cald Kilmaroy in Arisaig.
>
> Nixt to it ar the two Morroris perteyning to the Siell-Allan-Wick Rannald, on the southsyd or sumquhat west of LochMurour a fresche water Loch of sum four myles of lenth,

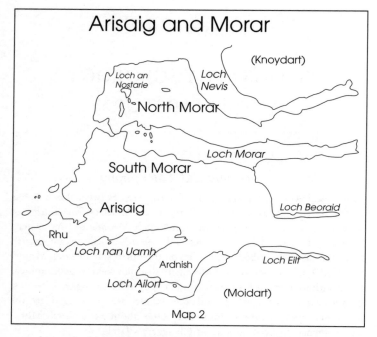

Arisaig and Morar

(Knoydart)

Loch an
Nostarie

Loch
Nevis

North Morar

Loch Morar

South Morar

Loch Beoraid

Arisaig

Rhu

Loch nan Uamh

Ardnish

Loch Eilt

Loch Ailort

(Moidart)

Map 2

and a myl of breadth which loch is compassed with hie moun-
taynes as also at the east head therof, all the countrey is rough
and montanous, with a river running from this Loch to the sea.

The uthir Morrour upon the northsyde of the Loch, pertaineth
to the Laird of Glengarry, a verie litle countrey, it hath fish,
bestial and pasture, but small stoar of cornis. Upon the northsyd
of this Morrour ther is a sealoch cumeth in betwixt both the
countreys of Morrour and Knodeart.

Macfarlane's Geographical Collections, Volume II, p 522

In 1700 Bishop Nicolson visited the area and points out the relative
advantages of the landscape in Arisaig which is described as

less hilly and more pleasant than Knoydart, Morar or Moydart,
which are all much the same in regard to rock and mountains
– whilst Arisaig is much more level and abounds in corn.

An anonymous author, probably David Bruce, gave a more sanguine
assessment in 1750:

All these Countries viz. Knoydart, the Two Morrirs, Moydart, and Arisag, are the most Rough Mountainous and impassable parts in all the Highlands of Scotland, and are commonly called by the Inhabitants of the Neighbouring Countries the Highlands of the Highlands. The People here have very little Corn Land and what they have by Reason of its steepness and Cragginess they are obliged to Dig with the Spade.

By spade David Bruce probably meant the *cas-chrom* which is a large angled foot-plough which allowed the user to turn over rough ground. A satellite photograph (see Plate 1) shows Arisaig's relative advantage in terms of the amount of flat land.

Geology

The bedrocks of the area are Moinian metamorphics like schist, mica-schist, and quartz. These are cut, particularly in South Morar and Arisaig, by igneous dykes of basalt and dolerite which run roughly North-South. In general such rocks prove intractable for agriculture but the area has also been affected by glacial action and the changing level of the sea. During the Ice Ages the Highlands were scoured by glaciers emanating from centres such as Rannoch Moor. At over 1000 feet deep, Loch Morar is the deepest loch in Britain and deeper than much of the surrounding sea until we reach the Atlantic shelf west of the Outer Hebrides. It was carved by such a glacier; a powerful and abrasive river of ice which ran East-West for most of its course but poured its outwash debris in a south-westerly direction from Camus Ruadh to Back of Keppoch. These outwash gravels are over-lain by a massive layer of peat called Mointeach Mhor (the Big Moss), the edges of which have been reclaimed for crofting.

The coastline was much affected by changing sea-levels during the Ice Ages. As the ice formed, so the sea-level fell; when the ice-sheets melted so the level of the surrounding seas rose. In turn the land lifted in response to the removal of the immense weight of ice. These fluctuations in sea-level have left extensive raised beaches, old sho-relines carved into the hillside high above the present reach of the tide. The remains of such beaches, cliffs and caves are visible around much of the coast, particularly at Ardnafuaran, Glasnacardoch and in the Morar Estuary.

This explains examples of marine deposition in places that are now

a long way from the sea. In 1868 Rev R Mapleton visited the site at
Loch nan Eala, Arisaig, where a crannog had been exposed by
drainage. His comments shed light on a previously higher sea-level:

> On the shores of the loch are evident marks of an old beach;
> and in the burn that fed the loch ... is an old sea-bottom, 2 feet
> above the present level of the loch, with 4 feet of peat lying
> above it. It is almost one mass of oyster-shells, with periwinkles
> and whelks, in a shallow bed of clay, above a layer of decayed
> land-plants, in which we saw several pieces of wood, apparently
> the branches of birch.

Similarly the Arisaig Scrapbook states that gravediggers reported a
great quantity of shells unearthed at the entrance to the cemetery.
Without excavation nothing further can be said but this might indicate
either a beach deposit or an ancient shell-midden.

In addition the sands created by the Atlantic have been cast up to
form dunes. These are now covered in grass and form the basis of
farms such as Traigh. The bedrock may not be amenable to agriculture
but glacial erosion, marine deposition and wind-blow have modified
the landscape to give pockets of good land, particularly along the
coastline from Cross to Back of Keppoch. The place-name Keppoch
(from Gaelic *ceapach*, arable land) itself confirms this since good soil
was always a noteworthy resource in the Highlands. The hinterland
has not been so softened and preserves its original rugged appearance.
Such a landscape amply justifies the old Gaelic name for the region
– *na Garbh Chriochan* – the Rough Bounds.

Prehistory

There are two ways to look at the prehistoric period in Arisaig and
Morar: either as an almost blank chapter in which we can do no
more than list those prehistoric monuments which have been discovered to date; or as an unopened treasure-chest for the future. For
the purposes of this book I am confined to the former, but on a
personal level remain optimistic about the latter. It is unlikely that
much more historical or documentary evidence will come to light but
it is to be hoped that one day our prehistoric monuments will be
properly investigated. Given the small resources of Highland
archaeologists and the large claims on their time, this may lie far
in the future. In the meantime the amateur can make a valuable

contribution to an understanding of past settlement by field-walking and the analysis of old estate papers, rentals and maps.

This is important because otherwise modern developments such as forestry can unwittingly damage the historic landscape. As I write this I am thinking of a long-abandoned, possibly mediaeval, farm by Loch an Nostarie. Across a neighbouring burn is a set of stepping-stones that is likely to be eighteenth-century or earlier. Sadly these have just been damaged by a forestry digger. This was plainly not intentional – the steps have never been officially recognised – but there is more history in our abandoned landscape than is visible at first sight and it may give pleasure in the future if we can recognise and preserve it. Ironically the very desolation of the Highlands has meant the preservation of an archaeological landscape which, in most other parts of Britain, has been lost to development.

Morar and Arisaig were, and are, distinct units but until the fragmentation of the Macruari estates in the fifteenth century they can be treated as one. They have always been a cultural unit but under the Macruaris, and perhaps for a long time previously, they were also a political unit. Nevertheless geographical considerations always set the tone for any discussion of the area's prehistory. It is clear that Arisaig is more favoured in agricultural terms than either North or South Morar. This is reflected in the distribution of prehistoric monuments and the density of settlement. Moreover the different communities had different orientations. The settlements on the north side of North Morar would have looked to Loch Nevis and Knoydart for contact; those on either shore of Loch Morar to each other, those in Arisaig south to Moidart or west to Eigg and Muck.

Although we can say something about the specific monuments that we find here, and although we can draw analogies from elsewhere about that class of monument in general, almost everything else is speculative. We can be sure of little with regard to the prehistoric period. We do not know what languages were spoken or what beliefs were followed. The population was never large; the economy was always pastoral with small areas under crop. They fished, hunted, and exchanged any surplus products with their richer neighbours. They lived short and hazardous lives.

This area was marginal in the sense of being less favoured, less prosperous and less secure. We know that its valuation in Norse, and probably Dalriadic, times was significantly lower than that of areas such as Glenelg, Sleat or Ardnamurchan. There is no reason to believe that general economic circumstances were very different in prehistoric times. Even under more favourable climatic conditions this area could never support much in the way of agriculture.

Prehistoric remains are categorised by classes of monument and periods of time. We talk of cairns and kists, crannogs and cup-marks. We use chronological labels like Stone or Bronze or Iron Age. Of necessity we must be loose in our definitions since different parts of the country could be at different stages of economic or technological development at the same moment of time. Nevertheless, in general terms, certain classes of monument or certain technologies are associated with specific periods. So the flint-chippings of a hunter-gatherer in Rum are said to be Mesolithic or Middle Stone Age whilst the chambered cairns of a farming community in Argyll are Neolithic or New Stone Age. Kists and cup-marks are termed Bronze Age whilst forts and duns are Iron Age.

What adds to the complexity is that lots of these sites, particularly forts, duns and crannogs, were physically occupied over very long periods of time. Since not a single prehistoric site in Arisaig or Morar has been properly excavated, we must be extremely flexible with our categories. What follows is brief, generalised, and purely for guidance. I have dealt with the prehistoric remains by class of structure within periods of time. Further references can be found in the National Monuments Record of Scotland which is maintained by the Royal Commission on the Ancient and Historical Monuments of Scotland and is available over the Internet.

Mesolithic or Middle Stone Age

In 1937 Dr Munro, an Inspector of Schools, sent A D Lacaille some stone artefacts which he had collected in Morar. Wartime restrictions prevented Lacaille from visiting the area until 1946, but then he investigated the beach himself and included references to it in his book *The Stone Age in Scotland*. Lacaille believed the beach-site to be the base for a group of hunter-gatherers who, because of their technology, could be called Mesolithic. Their tools and implements were mainly of quartz but about 60 flints were also found. Since flint does not occur naturally in Morar, it must have been brought from at least as far away as Mull or Morvern.

Prehistoric studies have advanced greatly in recent decades and the earliest evidence we now have for Mesolithic men in Scotland is from

Rum. This dates them back to *c.* 7000 BC. In the absence of a proper archaeological context it is impossible to date stray beach-finds of flint or quartz. Morar is either very ancient or it indicates the late survival of a people with archaic technological skills – in a location where the harsh environment delayed the development of agricultural society.

There are raised beaches all around Morar and at the back of them a number of caves. Many of these are full of debris but by analogy with similar sites elsewhere any, or all of them, could reveal traces of Mesolithic occupation. Tools and implements may be rare but shell-middens are often substantial and it would not surprise me if a great many more Mesolithic beach-sites await discovery. For example, a recent project in the Inner Sound of Raasay has identified up to three dozen new sites, though it is not yet certain whether they are all Mesolithic.

Flint is not local to this area, so any find of flint, or Rum bloodstone, suggests travel or commerce. A flint arrowhead was found on the shore at Red Sands Bay (Loch Morar) and another flint chip was found near Bracara. These are impossible to date but remind us that Morar was inhabited, even in the earliest times.

Neolithic or New Stone Age

The Neolithic period is associated with the fundamental economic change from groups of hunter-gatherers to settled farming communities. The latter developed the population and wealth to construct large-scale ritual monuments such as cairns and chambered cairns. In Arisaig two cairns have been reported at NM 664863 and NM 666855, near Mains Farm. They would require further investigation to confirm their age but this is certainly one of the most likely locations in the area.

Bronze and Iron Ages

It is impossible, in our area, to draw hard and fast distinctions between the so-called Bronze and Iron Ages. These were terms introduced many years ago to deal with the different metal-working technologies which, in certain areas, can be given meaningful time-frames. Whether they can in Morar and Arisaig, where prehistoric communities were probably primitive and marginal, is open to question. However, there are a number of monuments here which are normally associated with one or other of these periods (see Map 3).

Cairn and kist – Arisaig
A cairn containing a kist within a circular stone setting has recently been excavated in Arisaig.

Kist – Glen Mama
A short kist or stone-lined burial box was found in 1938 when making the new road at Glen Mama. The find-site is approximately NM 726844. The kist is now in the West Highland Museum.

Cup-marked stone – Ghaoideil
There is a cup-marked stone lying near the summit of the pass between Mains and Loch nan Uamh. It was described by William Jolly who visited the site in June 1881 accompanied by the teacher, the priest and the minister. The only local tradition they could discover was that

> it is said to possess certain virtues in connection with the ancient
> trade of the smith. When an apprentice smith washes his hands
> in the water that has fallen from the heavens into the large basin,
> at sunrise on the first day of May, it will impart peculiar cunning
> to his hand and strength to his arm!

Meagre though this tradition is, it provides more than enough for a thesis by any self-respecting folklorist. Is not 1 May the ancient Celtic festival of Beltane, the beginning of summer? Is not iron the only sure defence against fairy powers? Has not the craft of the smith something supernatural about it?

On a more prosaic note Jolly counted 82 cups carved into the stone and, in a nice tribute to Victorian thoroughness, got the priest and the teacher to go back and measure them for him! I spare you these details but give the reference in the Bibliography.

Iron Age

Forts and duns
The most visible Iron Age monuments in the West Highlands are the numerous forts and duns. Many of these were in use for so long that

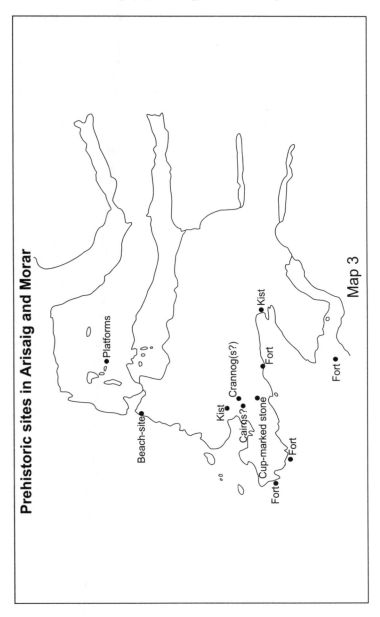

Prehistoric sites in Arisaig and Morar

Platforms

Beach-site

Kist

Crannog(s?)

Cairns?

Cup-marked stone

Fort

Fort

Fort

Kist

Fort

Fort

Map 3

their names have passed into the local toponymy, either in Gaelic or Norse form. We have Dunaverty, Dunollie and Dunvegan which include the word *dun* (Gaelic, fort) but also Borve and Borrodale which come from *borg* (Norse, fort). The very occurrence of the Norse place-name implies that these structures were maintained locally until the arrival of the first Vikings in the ninth century. We also know from the sagas that the Norse re-used the old duns and brochs as they required. The fort at Borrodale may have been the political headquarters of the local magnate, so what more natural than for the Norse invader to establish himself here?

The fort at Borrodale (NM 692840) has been given a variety of names such as Arka Unskel, Ard Ghamsghail etc. but these all seem to be corruptions of Aird (Point of) Camus nan Gall (Foreigners' Bay). It occupies a promontory below the present Arisaig House and is heavily vitrified, which means that the stones in the wall have melted and fused to form a concrete-like matrix. This is a common feature in West Highland forts and there has been a great deal of academic debate as to whether it was the result of accidentally firing the timber-laced ramparts or whether it was deliberate policy. At any rate the fort in Arisaig has walls that are still several feet high and thick, and was described by Christison, in 1898, as one of the best examples of a vitrified fort in Scotland.

In the New Statistical Account for Ardnamurchan, drawn up in 1838, Rev Angus M'Lean commented on the antiquities of the parish:

> Of these the most curious are, the vitrified forts, of which there are several, the largest and most remarkable being situated in Eilein nan Gobhar, in Lochaylort. On this islet ... are two works of this description, within a few yards of each other, one of an oblong figure, 140 paces in circumference, the other 90 paces and circular. The walls which, in some parts, are seven or eight feet high, are composed of stones of various sizes heaped confusedly, and cemented by vitrified matter, nowhere solid or compact. At the entrance to the largest, there are the remains of a facing of common stone imbedded in cement, which probably extended, at one time, all round the fort.

The walling on Eilean nan Gobhar is particularly impressive and is still visible from the road to Glenuig. It is probably this that James Hogg refers to in the course of his boat-trip from Irin to Arisaig in June 1804. There are other forts in the area. On the south side of the

Rhu peninsula are two islands which may have offered smaller-scale refuges. Eilean a' Ghaill (NM 627825) has a fort, while another fort has been claimed, and denied, for Eilean Port nam Murrach (NM 612835). On Eilean Ighe (NM 636881), off Gorten, are some enigmatic structures which may also represent a local stronghold. On the map we can see that the fortifications were in Arisaig, not Morar, and were coastal. The fact that they are on islands or promontories suggests that attack was expected from the land rather than the sea. They look like short-term refuges or bolt-holes.

Crannogs

Crannogs are lake or loch-houses. Over time many of these have simply slipped below the surface of the water where they escape attention. However, recent archaeological work suggests that they were common in the Highlands, and no doubt many more await discovery. What is extraordinary is their time-span. Some crannogs may date back to the Bronze Age and they were still being built at the end of the sixteenth century. An Act was passed in 1608 forbidding the building of crannogs, a sure sign that they were still in active use and that the authorities didn't like them.

About 1856 a crannog came to light in Loch nan Eala by Mains Farm. At an earlier period a canal had been dug to the sea, and the loch was now being drained. We have two accounts of the crannog: that by Rev Mapleton who visited the site in 1868 and another given by Blundell in 1911. This summary is drawn from both reports.

The crannog platform was rectangular, measuring 43' (13.11 m) by 41' (12.5 m). It was enclosed by sloping stays and consisted of several criss-crossed layers of wood, oak on top of birch. Some of these logs were substantial; Blundell measured an oak beam 53' (16.15 m) long and 30'' (.76 m) in circumference. Flagstones were found in three places, a piece of flint and some pieces of quartz. No causeway to the shore was discovered. There is little else we can say without excavation but even today the eroded tops of many of the stays are visible, as are some flagstones. Another smaller platform has been reported at NM 667857 on the south edge of the loch.

We have no historical evidence for this crannog but there is a local tradition that may represent the shadow of its presence. It was said of Clanranald that he could fish in Loch nan Eala from his bedroom window. Now of course this may simply refer to the former Clanranald mansion which stood beside what is now Glen Cottage –

formerly the servants' quarters. Before drainage, Loch nan Eala was substantially bigger and the loch may have come right below the windows of the house. However, it is just possible that in previous centuries the Clanranald chiefs, who often used to summer in Arisaig, actually occupied the crannog, in which case they could certainly have fished from a window. We do not yet know the precise occupation period of the Arisaig crannog but as late as 1580 Lachlan Mor Mackintosh built a crannog in Loch Lochy in order to subdue Lochaber.

Domestic structures

All the sites mentioned so far are ritual or defensive. We have very little to indicate how people lived ordinarily. While field-walking a few years ago I came across some unenclosed platforms which may turn out to be our earliest domestic sites. Often such platforms are dismissed as charcoal-burning structures but in the context here this seems unlikely. They lie beside Allt an t-Sean-achaidh and An-Leth-allt in North Morar. Now 'Sean-achaidh' literally means 'Old-field' and is on record from as early as 1762. If it was 'old' then, it is likely we are looking at a settlement that is at least mediaeval.

Despite their lack of fertile soil, the critical characteristics of these neighbouring valleys are remoteness and safety. North Morar was not a rich area but any settlement on the coast was vulnerable to sudden seaborne attack. The element of security may be the reason this area was favoured by earlier inhabitants. By the same token they may not be contemporary with the duns and forts which were built as coastal refuges.

Each site consists of a roughly circular platform, typically 8–12 metres by 5–9 metres in size. Generally the front of each platform is built up with several courses of stone (see Plate 2). There are four sites on the west bank of An Leth-allt with two more on the east side. All six are in close proximity to each other. It seems likely that the occupants were pastoral farmers since the banks of the burn are steep and they are not beside cultivable land. A few hundred metres away there are two more possible sites by Sean-achaidh. In a splash of sunshine these sites seem idyllic to modern eyes. Certainly they offered their occupants peace and security, if not plenty.

CHAPTER 2

EARLY CHRISTIANS AND VIKINGS

Early Christian

The definition of historic, as opposed to prehistoric, time is the presence of written records. For Arisaig and Morar these begin in the Early Christian period as the Irish monastic chronicles charted the progress of their missionary saints up the west coast of Scotland. We do not have their names for this district. Arisaig would not be so named until after the Norse arrived many years later. The most we have is a reference to an unnamed region which is probably Arisaig.

In 617 St Donnan and 52 of his monks were massacred at Kildonnan in Eigg, supposedly by a pagan from Arisaig. This good lady was chieftainess of the local tribe and took offence at the loss of her grazing lands in Eigg. These had evidently gone to the large new monastery at Kildonnan and so she ordered appropriately firm action. There are different versions of the story, one of the earliest of which, written about 800 AD, runs as follows:

> Donnan then went with his people to the Hebrides; and they took up their abode there, in a place where the sheep of the queen of the country were kept. This was told to the queen. 'Let them all be killed!' said she. 'It would not be a religious act,' said her people. But they were murderously assailed. At this time the cleric was at mass. 'Let us have respite till mass is ended,' said Donnan. 'Thou shalt have it,' said they. And when it was over, they were slain, every one of them.
>
> Martyrology of Oengus the Culdee, *c.* 800

The story is tantalising but inconclusive. During this period Eigg may have belonged to the adjacent mainland. We know from later evidence that Eigg and Arisaig both belonged to the same branch of the Macsorleys for at least 500 years. They may have been part of the same estate for hundreds of years previously as well. For reasons of geography the link is also more likely with Arisaig than Moidart.

Moreover this mainland society or tribe was headed by a queen, not a king, which invites parallels with the supposedly matrilineal nature of the Pictish royal family. We can do no more than speculate but the story does suggest that the monastery on Eigg represented a Christian Dalriadic intrusion into a pagan Pictish sphere of influence – which, in terms of the evidence from elsewhere, is exactly what we should expect. Moreover, like other, later religious reforms, it met with robust local opposition.

After this we have no further documentary clues as to the situation in Arisaig for the next six hundred years. However, we do have the place-name Kilmory which is on record from the early sixteenth century. The dedication of Kilmory is not to the Virgin Mary but, as is proven by its early spelling of Kilmaroy, to St Maelrubha. It is the *cill* or church of Maelrubha. Maelrubha is one of the most celebrated of the early missionary saints and founded the community at Apple-cross. He lived from 642 to 722. His foundation in Arisaig is thought to have been on the site of Keppoch Farm House, and certainly this is a favourable location, a south-facing aspect at the head of a sea-loch, near to cultivable ground.

At some stage in the Middle Ages, possibly in about the twelfth century with the development of the parish system, the church was moved up the hill to its present situation. However, the former site at Keppoch may still have been associated with religious maintenance because in later times the site was sometimes occupied by the priest. Nevertheless it remains puzzling why there is no surviving land-assessment unit which is specifically associated with religion. In many other areas of the West Highlands we find pennylands or quarterlands, even ouncelands, associated with churches, but not in Arisaig.

Kildonnan in Eigg was probably an ounceland or davach from around 600 AD when St Donnan first established his monastery there. Kilchoan in Knoydart was still a quarterland a thousand years after St Comgan founded and presumably endowed it. Either Kilmory in Arisaig had no original endowment or it had lost it. The church sank into relative obscurity; from which the Macsorleys seem to have rescued it in early mediaeval times by granting it parochial status.

The Early Christian site at Keppoch has so far yielded no relics, but Early Christian carved stones have been found in Knoydart and on each of the Small Isles. There is also an Early Christian hand-bell on Eilean Fhianain in Loch Shiel, Moidart. It is perfectly possible therefore that some early Christian carved stones remain to be uncovered in Arisaig. From other areas we know that these stones often suffered an inglorious fate. Some were re-used in dykes and walls, others were broken up or buried. They have come to light in all sorts of unlikely situations.

Even more difficult is to know whether the former graveyard in Morar preserves some memory of an ancient burial ground. It appears on the first Ordnance Survey map of the area as Cille Chuimein (the church of Cumine). This is also the Gaelic name for Fort Augustus, whilst an abbot of Iona called Cumine died in 669. Again, it is a likely site for a religious colonist: placed at the head of an estuary, by cultivable land which enjoys a south-facing aspect. It may once have housed a small missionary cell which never grew into a church but retained ritual significance as a burial ground.

There are a number of old graveyards in the Rough Bounds. In part these reflected necessity. In bad weather a body could not be carried far by land or sea. Accordingly there are burial grounds on Eilean Tioram at the head of Loch Nevis, at Cille Chuimein, North Morar, at the mouth of the River Meoble in South Morar, at Kilmory, Arisaig, and on a small island in the River Ailort. It is impossible to know how old these are and whether they are Christian or pagan in origin. One of the main purposes of burial has always been to preserve the corpse from scavenging animals such as wolves, and it is probably for this reason that island sites were favoured.

There is also the enigma of the place-name Cross. This is on record from 1610 when the farms on the South Morar estate are listed. High crosses were often erected by leading families during the Middle Ages although many were destroyed in the sixteenth and more especially the seventeenth centuries. It is therefore likely that the place-name Cross predates the Reformation. It may be relevant that the South Morar estate was held by a family who also owned about one-third of Eigg. This small but valuable island had at least four mediaeval high crosses.

The Norse

We know there was extensive Norse colonisation of the Hebrides and mainland west coast but we have little tangible evidence. For Arisaig and Morar we have no documentary records, no archaeological sites and no surviving buildings. Virtually everything we say about the Norse presence here depends upon evidence drawn from elsewhere. So how can we be sure they were here at all? Because we can see their legacy in place-names and the land-assessment system.

Place-names

Place-names like Scamadale are plainly Norse since it is composed of two Norse words *skammr* (short) and *dalr* (dale) – which is exactly what it is. The second element has passed into English as dale and Gaelic as *dail*. However the first element *skammr* was not borrowed by Gaelic which uses the word *gearr* instead – as in Gairloch (short loch), Kingairloch, Garelochhead etc. The name Scamadale must have had a meaning for its first users, but once these Norse speakers had died out its meaning was lost to the subsequent Gaelic-speaking inhabitants. Nevertheless it remained in local use long enough for the name to become fixed, and survive, even after it ceased to have a literal meaning.

By extension this argument could be applied to every Norse name in the area. They would not be with us today if they had only been names known to seasonal visitors. Instead they were maintained and passed on by local Gaelic populations because they had been inherited as part of the local linguistic set. They had been absorbed into the district consciousness, as names rather than words, over a considerable period of time. Such a local toponymy is unlikely to have been established in less than three generations.

When tracing derivations, the place-name researcher must always look for the earliest possible written evidence. In our area this is found in a handful of thirteenth- and fourteenth-century charters. The name Arisaig is recorded as Arasech in 1250 (albeit in a later copy), as Araseg *c.* 1325 and as Aresayg in 1343. The name Morar appears as Mordowor *c.* 1325 and as Mordhower in 1343. Both names are simple descriptions. Arisaig is Norse and means 'river-mouth bay'; Morar is Gaelic and means 'big water'.

To begin with the only names recorded are the district-names but as time moves on we learn the names of actual settlements. In *c.* 1309 we hear of Gedeuall (Ghaoideil), Glenbestell (Glen Beasdale) and Bethey (Torr a' Bheithe?) in Ayrsayk (Arisaig). Such names accumulate in subsequent centuries. Some of these, like Aucholledill and Fertacorrie, are now lost. Others such as Creive, Nakyrsyde and North Blyth are corrupt and initially unrecognisable.

All these early names are of districts or settlements. The latter are particularly important since they represent the mediaeval townships and farm-units – of which later names are often extensions or sub-divisions. We do not learn of topographical or landscape names until much later. But from the eighteenth century we have maps, rentals and numerous written accounts, all of which add to our place-name stock. We have a short list of names in North Morar which, although nineteenth-century in form, probably represents a mental map taken to Canada by emigrants in 1786. We also have the maps resulting from General Roy's military survey of the area (1747–55), which help us physically locate our names. These maps include not only the 'Fair Copy', which is well-known, but the lesser-known and in some ways more informative 'Protracted Copy' or rough draft. From the end of the nineteenth century we have the first Ordnance Survey maps, and alongside them the Name Books in which local derivations were recorded.

People will always try and interpret names, whether they be occu-piers, visitors or historians. This happens in the early Icelandic sagas; David Bruce did it in Arisaig in 1748; and we are still doing it today. We are intrigued by the question of how names occurred, what they signify. We are not content with a function, we require a meaning as well. Sometimes we produce a convincing explanation, but the further back we go, the more difficult it becomes. Names from one language are gradually transformed by the speakers of another – Norse names by the Gaels, Gaelic names by the Scots. Norse names can appear Gaelic whilst names from either language can be 'rationalised' by later residents as their own contribution. (By this we mean a process where a name is justified or explained to users of a new language in their own terms. This may involve a modification to its original meaning.)

A good example of the metamorphosis involved in rationalisation is Greenhill in Tiree. This name probably started off life as the Norse *groen-vollr* (green-field). The second element occurs in another Tiree name, Mannal, whose early forms prove it to be a *vollr* name. Over time *vollr* became modified on the west coast to *-al*, giving Grianal. More recently this name has been modified again and on the Ordnance Survey map we find 'Greenhill House' which, presumably, satisfies the requirements of a current linguistic process. Given that nowhere in the immediate landscape is much more than 20 metres above sea level, it is unlikely that 'Greenhill' reflects its original Norse meaning.

Nevertheless 'Greenhill' it is, and once a name is fixed on a map its permanence is more assured. For these reasons we must be very cautious when assigning meanings to names.

We have a local example of such difficulties in the place-name Loch Ailort. Our earliest spellings come from a series of sixteenth-century maps by Ortelius (1573), Leslie (1578), Nicolay (1583) and Mercator (1595). These all spell the loch 'Enzord' (where 'z' sounds as 'y'), although it is difficult to know whether they derived the name from a common source. The documentary record shows more variety. There is Kinlochaylort (1613), Kenloch haynard (1699), Alliard (1746), Kinlochaliort (1748), Ailleart (Alexander Macdonald, poet), Halliort (Roy *c.* 1755), and Kinloch-Enort (1804), whilst the minister of Ardnamurchan parish in 1838 refers to it promiscuously as Lochainart *and* Lochaylort. Both versions have long pedigrees and there are other Loch Eynorts on the west coast. Were these names just two different renderings of the one sound?

There is a further issue over the process we should adopt when analysing place-names. We have written records, we have maps, and we have the names as they survive in everyday speech. In the case of variance, which type of evidence should we prefer? Now there is no doubt that a twenty-first-century Gaelic pronunciation is always to be preferred to a twenty-first-century English one. This is not such a compelling argument when the Scots or English version is eighteenth-century and given by someone who either spoke or had a good knowledge of Gaelic. For instance, the place-name Samadalan in Knoydart is explained by two nineteenth-century residents as the 'Stinking Dales' – from the piles of seaweed rotting on the shore. Yet in 1637 the same name is recorded as Sandland where the words signify exactly what they do in English, which, like Norse, is a Germanic language. Similarly, it is difficult to equate the present English spelling of Knoydart with a Gaelic pronunciation of the same word, and yet it compares very well with the name as spelt in our earliest charters.

The name Meoble has often been cited as including the Norse element *bolstadr* or farm. As such it has particular importance as one of the very few Norse farm-sites on the mainland west coast. It has recently been argued that the element it contains is actually Gaelic *-poll* or pool. Yet in three seventeenth-century charters it is spelled with a 'b' whilst in 1747 Ned Burke, a Gaelic-speaker who spoke Scots very badly, refers to it as Mewboll. In the same way another local

-*bol* name – Polnish – is written as Bullneish in 1748. Again, any railway passenger can tell you that you catch a train from Glasgow to Mallaig (stress on second syllable) but actually arrive in a place called Mallaig (stress on first syllable). Now whilst there are far more Glaswegians than people in Mallaig the latter pronunciation is likely to be closer to the original. The modification and transformation of names continues today.

All of these difficulties make place-name studies a minefield. There is seldom proof, merely a balance of probabilities, and there can be no resolution of some of the arguments about origin. The best we can offer is a list of names drawn from the earliest available sources and give all the different forms we can find. We can then suggest derivations based on likely meaning, an understanding of the local topography and parallels drawn from elsewhere.

This last is an important and often overlooked point. It is striking how often place-names recur in different parts of the Rough Bounds. There are Scamadales by Loch Shiel, Loch Morar, and in Knoydart; Sandaigs in Arisaig and Knoydart; Bourblachs in Ardnamurchan, Morar and Glenelg; Swordlands in Morar and Glenelg. These repetitions suggest we have similar groups of people settling similar areas of land and naming them in similar terms.

For all these reasons Map 4 is no more than a cautious and provisional summary of the Norse contribution. It represents probability rather than knowledge. Nevertheless it is important to draw attention to place-names because so many are currently being lost or indiscriminately replaced.

Settlement and Influence

The place-name evidence is used by historians in the continuing debate about the extent and depth of Norse settlement on the west coast. There is a minimalist perspective which regards Norse names on the mainland as the result merely of seasonal occupation or influence. In particular there is a great shortage of 'habitative' names, i.e. those indicating permanent and fixed accommodation. The argument goes that only 'habitative' names such as *bolstadr* or *settr* can prove settlement, all other names merely provide circumstantial evidence. In the absence of any material or archaeological remains such an argument is difficult to disprove. Can we accumulate evidence to the contrary?

Although Norse 'habitative' names are generally scarce on the west

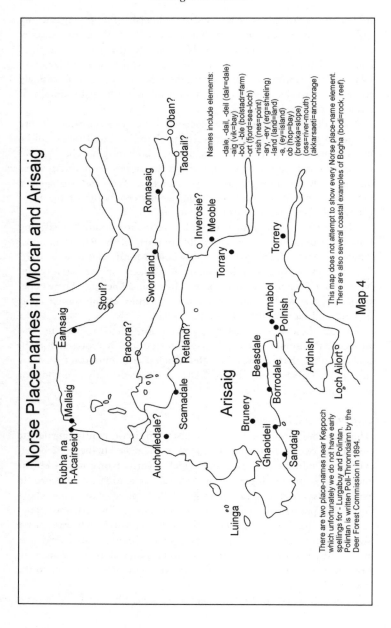

Norse Place-names in Morar and Arisaig

Rubha na
h-Acairseid • Mallaig

Earnsaig •

Stoul?

Bracora?

Swordland

Romasaig •

Oban? ○

Taodail? ○

Auchojedale? •

Scamadale •

Retland? •

Inverosie? ○

Meoble •

Torrary •

Torrery •

Bracora?

Arisaig

Brunery

Beasdale •

Borrodale •

Ghaoideil •

Sandaig •

Arnabol •
Polnish •

Ardnish

Loch Ailort ○

Luinga

Names include elements:

-dale, -dail, -deil (dalr=dale)
-aig (vik=bay)
-bol, -ble (bolstadr=farm)
-ort (fjord=sea-loch)
-nish (nes=point)
-ary, -ery (erg=shieling)
-land (land=land)
-a, (ey=island)
ob (hop=bay)
(brekka=slope)
(oss=river-mouth)
(akkarsaeti=anchorage)

This map does not attempt to show every Norse place-name element.
There are also several coastal examples of Bogha (bodi=rock, reef).

Map 4

There are two place-names near Keppoch
which unfortunately we do not have early
spellings for – Lurgabuy and Polintain.
Polintain is written Poll-Thronndainn by the
Deer Forest Commission in 1894.

coast, they do exist, particularly in this area. There are two *bolstadr* names – Meoble, South Morar, and Arnabol in Arisaig. (Polnish is probably just an extension of Arnabol.) There are also other place-name elements such as *land* or *vollr* which add weight to the argument for a strong Norse presence. *Land* (land) is a common enough farm-name in the far north of Scotland and is found in North Morar as Swordland, Knoydart as Sandland and Glenelg as Suardelan. Swordland is the more persuasive because the Norse first element *svard* (sward) is common along the west coast and in Skye (Suardal etc.).

Vollr (field) is more difficult. It, too, is common in the far north where it becomes the ending -well or -wall in names such as Langwell or Dingwall. Along the west coast and in the Hebrides it is more usually contracted to -al. Thus we find Langal (Bute and Moidart), Grianal and Mannal (Tiree). In fact the Moidart Langal is recorded as Languell in a document composed in 1745. This is a roll of Moidart men who served in Clanranald's regiment, and since it lists them under the various farms it seems fair to assume this represents a current local pronunciation. There is one name in our district which just conceivably includes the element *vollr* and that is Stoul. In John Macdonald's list from Canada, which represents the toponymy of 1786, we find Stoal, and it is possible that the second element is a contraction of *vollr*.

Certain Norse words like *land*, *dalr* and *ob/hop* passed into Gaelic as loan words and their presence only proves influence rather than settlement. However, the sheer quantity of Norse names, their pro-portion to the overall toponymy, and their presence throughout our area, inland as well as on the coast, all suggest a strong Norse input. The fact that some names include Norse elements which did not pass into Gaelic confirms that they must have become fixed in the local linguistic set over a long period of time. As a result they became absorbed as names even when they were meaningless as words. If we accept the Norse presence as outlined on Map 4, can we put geo-graphical limits on it? Where was its eastern boundary?

It is generally held that Norse settlement did not reach as far east as the Great Glen. However, there is a cluster of Norse names at the north end of Loch Linnhe and no doubt there was significant trade and communication down the Great Glen at the times of greatest Norse power. In abstract geographical terms we might expect the eastern limit of Norse expansion from the west coast to be at the watershed to the east of the coastal glens. Up to this limit they were within reach of reinforcement or evacuation by sea. Beyond this they were dangerously exposed. Is there any evidence to support this notional frontier?

There is one place-name which may help us. The Gaelic word for foreigner is *Gall* which in recent centuries has been used in the context of Lowland Scots. Before this it was often used of Scandinavians, which is how we get names like Innsegall (Foreigners' Isles) for the Hebrides as well as personal names like Fingal and Dougal. Down the west coast we find numerous examples of Eilean nan Gall (Foreigners' Isle), Camus nan Gall (Foreigners' Bay), Rubha nan Gall (Foreigners' Point) etc.

Theoretically these *Gall* could be Scots or English foreigners but in such cases the incursions tend to be relatively recent and we can sometimes tell from the context in which the names occur. We may know something particular about the history of a place (e.g. fishing or industrial activity) or the place-name may be specific and state Albannach (Scotsman) or Sasunnach (i.e. Saxon or Englishman) – as do two neighbouring hills in South Morar. In the case of *Gall*, though, many of these coastal names probably date back 1000 years to the period when the Norse were the foreigners and when certain coastal localities were particularly identified with them. So the Camus nan Gall at Borrodale was probably given its name when the first Norse settlers established themselves in the Iron Age fort on the shore.

There are three place-names called Coire nan Gall (see Map 5) which run virtually north-south between the head of Loch Duich and the head of Loch Shiel. These are remote and isolated hill pastures whose names are not of the type that occur in early charters and land-grants. Both Norse and Gael practised transhumance and took their livestock up to the high pastures in the summer.

In other Highland areas, such as the uplands of Banffshire and Aberdeenshire, there was an old practice of taking in *gall* cattle (i.e. the cattle of strangers) for summer pasturage. This is unlikely to be the reason for the place-name here because this area was extremely isolated and the corries concerned are very remote. Moreover, one of them, Coire nan Gall between Knoydart and Loch Arkaig, is recorded under the name Corrinangaull as early as 1747, well before there was any significant Lowland or English presence in the area.

It seems possible that all three corries refer in fact to the summer pastures of Norse farms. These would be situated at the eastern

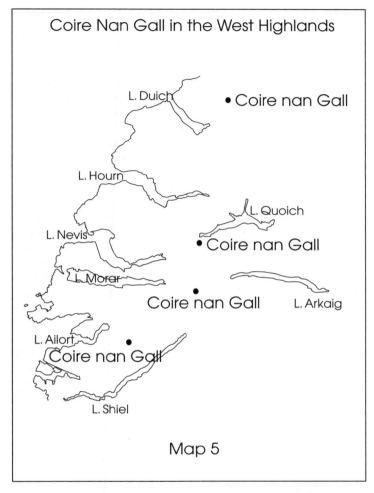

Coire Nan Gall in the West Highlands

L. Duich

• Coire nan Gall

L. Hourn

L. Quoich

L. Nevis

• Coire nan Gall

L. Morar

Coire nan Gall

L. Arkaig

L. Ailort •

Coire nan Gall

L. Shiel

Map 5

extremities of Norse settlement – along the watershed east of the coastal fjords. This boundary may have been relatively stable for the period of active Norse colonisation, long enough for the place-name to become fixed in the local spatial set.

There are other Coire nan Galls, for instance in Moidart, which do not so obviously fit this north-south pattern, but these three may give us a border for Norse settlement in our area. The seaborne migrants would colonise along the shores of the sea-lochs – Duich, Hourn and Nevis – and to the watershed behind. Loch Morar was almost as accessible as a sea-loch because the crossing from Loch Nevis at Tarbert is so narrow that light boats could easily be drawn across. (This is what the place-name Tarbert signifies – a portage point where a narrow piece of land intervenes between two stretches of water.) As a result Norse settlers could reach the eastern end of Loch Morar as well as Loch Beoraid. This would explain the cluster of Norse names around Loch Morar and at Meoble.

We would not expect the Norse to reach into the hinterland. Once they had crossed the watershed to the east, they were out of their own domain and into enemy territory. Moreover this was territory that could be defended in depth and where the Norsemen themselves were beyond the reach of rapid reinforcement from the sea. If the Norse did not arrive in huge numbers, it is perfectly understandable that they confined themselves to an easily defended coastal strip, a strip which they could reinforce from the sea or from which they could escape by boat if necessary. They probably pushed the in-digenous peoples east to the head of Loch Morar and then through the hill passes by Glen Pean and Glen Dessary to Loch Arkaig and the Great Glen.

Land-Assessment

One of the characteristics of the areas of Norse settlement in Scotland is the unique system of land-assessment which is found here. The system is in terms of two units, ouncelands and pennylands, which may not have originated at the same time. (On the west coast an ounceland consisted of twenty pennylands.) To complicate matters, the Norse system was superimposed on an earlier Pictish or Dalriadic system of davachs. The davach was the functional equivalent of an ounceland, and we have a charter of Robert the Bruce (*c.* 1309) which refers to both davachs and pennylands in the context of Arisaig.

Map 6 gives the pennyland assessment of Morar and Arisaig. In general terms it seems that North and South Morar were worth 12*d* each whilst the Arisaig estate was worth 30*d*. Ardnish and a strip of land running east to Essan and Ranachan seem to have been regarded as separate and were worth at least 4*d* at one time. Morar and Arisaig, plus Ardnish, were probably worth three ouncelands originally. They were part of the eight ouncelands of Garmoran which also included Moidart and Knoydart.

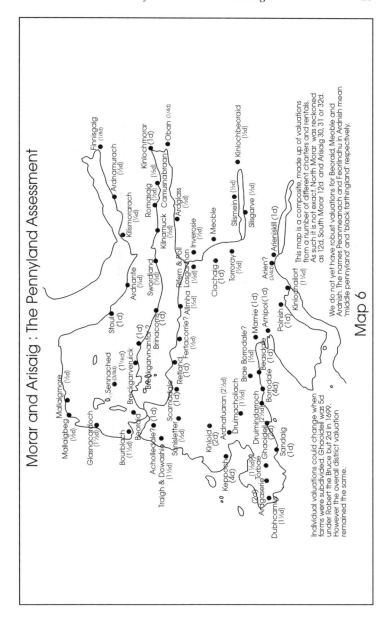

Morar and Arisaig : The Pennyland Assessment

Finnisgaig (1/8d)
Ardnamurach (¼d)
Kinlochmorar (1d)
Killismororach (¼d)
Romasaig (½d)
Kinlochmorar
Oban (1/4d)
Kilnamuck Camusnabraan
Camusnabraan
Ardglass (½d)
Meoble
Kinlochbeoraid (½d)
Slismein (½d)
Slisgarve (¼d)
Swordland (½d)
Ardnante (¼d)
Inverosie (½d)
Retan & Poll
Losgaicon
Torroray (½d)
Stoul (1d)
Clachaig (1d)
Brinacortie
Breckgarvanton ?
Breckgarveuick (1d)
Fertacorrie ? Alimha
Fertacorrie ? (1d)
Retland (½d)
Arien ? (3/4d)
Arieniskill (1d)
Kinlochnallort (1½d)
Polnish (1d)
Mamie (1d)
Arnipol (1d)
Beasdale (1d)
Brae Borrodale ?
Borrodale (4d)
Sennached (1½d)
Mallaigmore (½d)
Mallaigbeg (½d)
Beoraid (1½d)
Scamadale (1d)
Bourblach (1½d)
Glasnacardoch (1½d)
Achollectle ? (1d)
Stanisletter (1d)
Ardnafuaran (2½d)
Traigh & Dowashie (1½d)
Druimindarroch (1½d)
Druimachollaich (1d)
Ghaoidell (2d)
Kinloid (2d)
Keppoch (4d)
Torbae (2d)
Anggaserie (1½d)
Ghaoidell
Sandaig (1d)
Dubhcamhs (1½d)

This map is a composite, made up of valuations from a number of different charters and rentals. As such it is not exact. North Morar was reckoned as 12d. South Morar 12d and Arisaig 30, 31 or 32d.

We do not yet have robust valuations for Beoraid, Meoble and Ardnish. The names Peanmeanach and Feorlindhu in Ardnish mean 'middle pennyland' and 'black farthingland' respectively.

Individual valuations could change when farms were subdivided. Ghaoidell was 5d under Robert the Bruce but 2d in 1699. However the overall district valuation remained the same.

Map 6

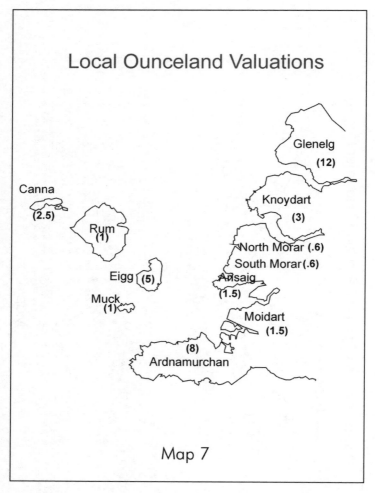

Local Ounceland Valuations

Glenelg
(12)

Canna
(2.5)

Knoydart
(3)

Rum
(1)

North Morar **(.6)**

South Morar **(.6)**

Eigg **(5)**

Arisaig
(1.5)

Muck
(1)

Moidart
(1.5)

(8)
Ardnamurchan

Map 7

This assessment is useful in allowing us to establish the relative worth of the district in Norse times. For comparison Map 7 shows the values of some neighbouring areas, and it is immediately obvious that the Rough Bounds were always regarded as impoverished.

Conclusions

This area was thoroughly mixed. Ninth-century Irish chronicles talk of the Gall-Gaidil occupying the Hebrides. These people were of mixed Norse-Gaelic descent and were regarded by the monks as even more savage than the Vikings themselves. We know the ingredients of this mix but not much about the proportions or the process. In truth these factors probably varied from area to area. The Northern Hebrides, particularly Lewis and Skye, had a very large percentage of Norse settlers. On the mainland, as you would expect, the process of settlement and colonisation was more ambiguous.

We do not even know if the existing population was Gaelic or Pictish or, conceivably, neither. Whoever they were, they could always retreat to the east rather than face extinction. In some cases the incomers probably evicted local families from the better land and drove their members into lower-status positions as tenants or servants. In other situations they may well have intermarried with local dynasties in order to ensure their own legitimacy and survival. The resulting amalgam was set by 1250. The district names for this area tell us of its mixed ancestry and composition. Working from north to south, we have Glenelg (Gaelic), Knoydart (Norse), Morar (Gaelic), Arisaig (Norse), Moidart (Norse), Sunart (Norse) and Ardnamurchan (Gaelic). Within each of these districts the names are a similar composite.

CHAPTER 3

THE MIDDLE AGES

Arisaig and Morar have always had an economic, social and cultural identity, and until about 1500 they shared a political identity as well. From at least the early thirteenth century they were owned by the Macruari family, one of the three great branches of Somerled's kin who dominated the western seaboard from the 1150s (see Figure 1). The Macruaris appear to have been pushed out of their estates in Kintyre and south Argyll in the 1220s and then moved north to establish, or relocate to, a power-base in the Rough Bounds. Two of the oldest families in Kintyre are the MacEachans and the MacEacherns. Both these family names are found in the Arisaig area, and although other derivations have been offered, it is possible they came with the Macruaris in the thirteenth century.

During the thirteenth century the Macruaris were very pro-Norse and may even have held kingship over the Northern Hebrides in the 1250s. They actively supported King Hakon's great expedition of 1263, but after the Treaty of Perth in 1266 they had to make their accommodation with Scotland. By 1343 the Macruaris were Lords of Garmoran, which included Moidart, Arisaig, Morar and Knoydart. This was the territory of *garbh* or rough Morvern in contrast to the more favoured area of Morvern itself. In addition to this huge swathe of territory they also held the islands of Eigg, Rum, Uist, Barra and St Kilda. After various accidents and political misfortunes the family estates devolved to a woman, Amy Macruari, who had married, in 1337, her cousin John of Islay. In this way the lands of two branches of Somerled's family were reunited and the primacy of the Islay branch was assured.

On John's death in 1380 his Macruari estates fell to his children by Amy – Reginald (whose family were thenceforward known as Clanranald), and Godfrey. With each succeeding generation there was of course the question of how the lands were to be divided between

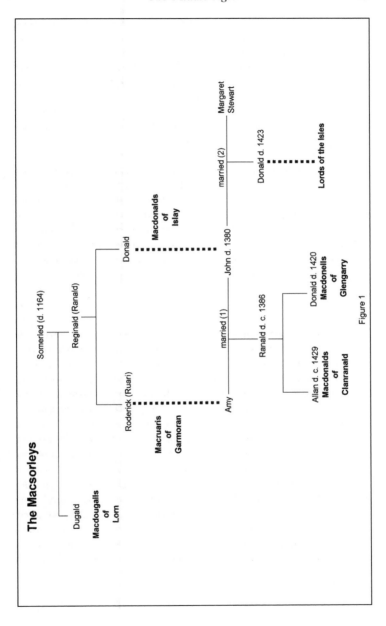

The Macsorleys

Somerled (d. 1164)

Dugald
Macdougalls of Lorn

Reginald (Ranald)

Roderick (Ruari)
Macruaris of Garmoran

Donald
Macdonalds of Islay

Amy
married (1)
John d. 1380
married (2)
Margaret Stewart

Donald d. 1423
Lords of the Isles

Ranald d. c. 1386

Allan d. c. 1429
Macdonalds of Clanranald

Donald d. 1420
Macdonells of Glengarry

Figure 1

the heirs, which explains how various parts of the Macruari estate were subsequently hived off. About 1429 Knoydart was detached to the family of Allan, second son of Allan of Clanranald. The South Morar estate is recorded from 1498 although it was always closely associated with Clanranald. Arisaig remained with Clanranald but by 1501 the lands of North Morar had passed to the family of Glengarry. None of the details of this process are clear. In fact, at the beginning of the nineteenth century there was a bitter dispute over precedence between the Glengarry and Clanranald families.

This gradual dismemberment of the Macruari estate, this process of disintegration, is important insofar as it affected the political history of the area. In social, economic and cultural terms life went on just as before. The people on either side of Loch Morar intermarried and exchanged goods as they had always done. It was just that the political focus for North Morar had now shifted from Castle Tioram in Moidart to Invergarry in the Great Glen. Generally the two great branches of Macranald or Ranaldson, as they were called, marched in the same political direction, but the details started to differ.

North Morar

Our earliest description of North Morar gives it as 'a verie litle countrey'. This implies it had little significance in economic or political terms. Its rugged geography meant that it was agriculturally poor and therefore worth only 12d to the landowner, compared to 30d for Arisaig or 60d for Knoydart. Its population probably never rose above about 350. It had no community of any size, no church, and made no visible cultural contribution. It just consisted of a scatter of houses along the shores of Loch Nevis, Loch Morar, and around Loch an Nostarie. It produced men, cattle, and some rent, probably mainly in kind. Its settlement pattern followed its pennyland assessment. This assessment is probably a good indicator of habitation from at least Dalriadic times. The less favoured inland areas only came under pressure with population expansion in the eighteenth century. Since no buildings survive from the mediaeval period, only field-walking and reading the agricultural pattern will reveal anything. North Morar remained of little strategic importance until the second half of the nineteenth century and the development of the herring industry.

We have one piece of evidence which shows us how clan feuds could occasionally make an impact on even such a remote area. In

Sir R Gordon's *History of Sutherland* there is a description of a feud between the Mackenzies and the Macdonells of Glengarry in 1602. Glengarry, then the owner of North Morar, was apparently 'unexpert and unskilfull in the lawes of the realme'. Mackenzie secretly charged him, had him denounced as a rebel and outlawed, and then secured a commission against him:

> Mackeinzie, being assisted by the nighbouring cuntries, by vertue of his commission, went into Morall [Morar], and spoilled Glengary his cuntrey, wasting and destroying the same with fyre and suord at his pleasure.

Such a raid could mean economic disaster locally. The loss of cattle might not be made good for years.

South Morar

South Morar and Arisaig were not physically separated in the way that North Morar was by Loch Morar. The farms of South Morar abutted those of Arisaig, so the contacts were many and frequent. Like North Morar, these lands were originally part of the old Macruari estate but it is important to distinguish between South Morar the district, and the South Morar estate. They were not always coterminous. At the time of the '45 the owner's family was still closely associated with Clanranald. Macdonald of Morar was second-in-command of the Clanranald regiment.

Local families tended to reinforce their positions, and safeguard their estates, by a careful process of dynastic intermarriage. Each generation tried to maintain the integrity of the family and its land against the natural process of subdivision. With each new generation children had to be provided for. When a line died out, the land could be clawed back. This process continued until the nineteenth century when the whole Clanranald patrimony finally fell apart.

The pennyland assessment in South Morar closely matched that of North Morar, and although its hills are a little higher, its economy and society must have been very similar. The estate of South Morar is on record from 1498 when it is described as a 14 merkland. The lands are not specified in 1498 but they are in a number of charters and retours from the seventeenth century. These names are set out in Figure 2, where it is plain what desperate corruptions could take place when clerks copied from each other. The lists are essentially

The Estate of South Morar

RMS VII (264) March 1610	RMS VII (344) July 1610	Retours (Inverness, 47) September 1627	RMS IX (7) January 1634	RMS XI (1105) October 1667	Retours (Inverness, 118) December 1695	Modern Name
Cros	Croce	Crae	Croce	Crock	Creive	Cross
Tray	Tray	Tray	Tray	Tray	Tray	Traigh
Duassiche	Duassich	Duassich	Duassich	Dowasick	Dowassick	(Allt an) Dubh-Asaidh
Aucholledill	Aucholladill	Aucholadill	Aucholladill	Ocholaddill	Auchollandick	
Schunisletir	Schonnisletir	Schomusletter	Schoinischeter	Scounshettar	Scomishettir	Sunisletter
Scammodill	Skammodill	Skammadill	Skaimodill	Scamadill	Skumadill	Scamadale
Raittalane	Raittillane	Ratulian	Raittillain	Raitillin	Rattallin	Retland
Fertacorrie	Ferracorie	Ferratorie	Ferracorie	Ferourie	Phirourie	? (Lettermorar)
Clachak	Clachik	Clachock	Clachik	Clathick	Clathick	Clachaig
Inverossie	Inverrossie	Inneroussie	Inverrossie	Inneressick	Inneressig	(Inverosie)
Mevybill	Merybill	Merrikillie	Merrybill	Merybill	Merikill	Meoble
Lochbored	Lochbore	Lochbeoraid	Lochbore	Lochbore	Lochbore	Loch Beoraid
Worblaich	Worthblach	Worklach	Worthblaich	North Bethe	North Blyth	Bourblach
Archicharre	Arichicharrie	Arrichicharrie	Arichicharrie	Arrichicharie	Arichicharie	Airidh a Choire/Eireagoraidh
Nakarsaid	Naikersad	Nakyrsyde	Naikersaid	Naikerfaid	Nackerfaid	Na h-Acairseid
Pouliskinane	Pouliskinane	Pouliskman	Polskuman	Pauliskinan	Poulistman	Poll Losgannan
14 m	14 m	14 m	14 m	14 m	14 m	
Morowre	Morrour	Morrour	Morrour	Morrour	Morrour	Morar

Aucholledill and Fertacorrie are now lost and appear on no map. Inverossie does not appear on modern maps but is marked by Roy.

RMS = Registrum Magni Sigilli Regum Scotorum (Register of the Great Seal of Scotland), Edinburgh, 1984.
Retours = Inquisitionum ad Capellam Domini Regis Retornatarum, 3 vols, London, 1811-1816.

Figure 2

the same in all 6 documents, and because the overall assessment was still 14 merklands, it seems reasonable to assume that this estate was unchanged since 1498. The earliest documents are clearly the most accurate – between 1610 and 1695 Worblaich had become North Blyth! In fact only one name – Tray (Traigh) – remains the same throughout.

Fortunately, like many other charters, the list of settlements runs in a geographically coherent manner – in this case from west to east up the south side of Loch Morar. Most of the names are still recognisable today although Aucholledill and Fertacorrie have disappeared. Certain settlements on Loch Morar are not mentioned – principally Almha and the stretch from Meoble to Oban which included Ardglas and Glen Taodhail. It may be that these patches of ground had been subsumed under the names of other settlements, or they may not have been part of the same estate. (See Map 8 and Plate 3).

Another anomaly is that the South Morar estate seems to include three names from North Morar. Worblaich is Bourblach (the Bourblach in Glenelg is spelled Worblache in a retour of 1608). Nakarsaid is an anglicised version of the Gaelic *Na h-Acairseid* (the anchorage) and refers to the harbour of Mallaigveag which is now the village of Mallaig. This leaves us with Archicharre. The earliest charter is misleading here. All the other documents suggest that the first element is Ari-, i.e. *airidh* or shieling. This is the same word which the Norse borrowed as *-erg* and then used in place-names with the ending -ary or -ery (Brunery, Torrery etc.).

The place-name Archicharre is probably what is now marked on the maps as Eireagoraidh. This name is puzzling but on the earliest Ordnance Survey map of the area in 1873 it is written *Airidh a' Choire* – literally the shieling of the corrie – which is perfectly descriptive. Eireagoraidh forms a great natural bowl with a grassy sward on the north shore of the loch where there are more than twenty old shieling huts. It has a narrow entrance so that herding cattle would be very simple. In time of danger it would also be very safe. From the point of view of access it is the obvious shieling for farms between Bourblach and Mallaig.

The question which arises is – why does the Clanranald estate of South Morar possess part of the Glengarry estate of North Morar? Our first reference to Glengarry ownership dates to 1501 when Alexander of Glengarry is summoned before the Privy Council for

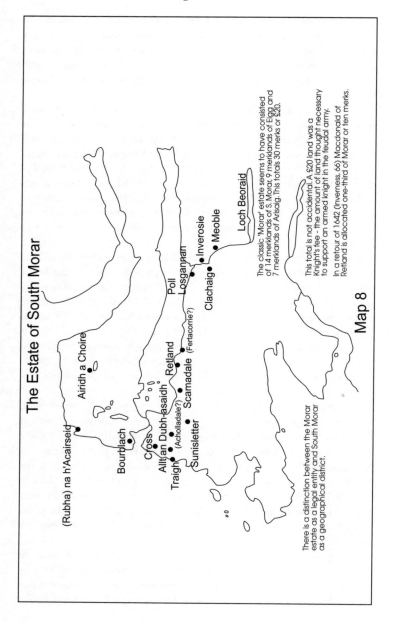

The Estate of South Morar

(Rubha) na h'Acairseig

Airidh a Choire

Bourblach

Cross

Allt an Dubh-asaidh

Traigh

(Achalladale?)

Sunisletter

Scamadale

Retland

(Fertacorrie?)

Poll

Losganan

Clachaig

Inverosie

Meoble

Loch Beoraid

The classic 'Morar' estate seems to have consisted of 14 merklands of S. Morar, 9 merklands of Eigg and 7 merklands of Arisaig. This totals 30 merks or £20.

This total is not accidental. A £20 land was a Knight's fee – the amount of land thought necessary to support an armed knight in the feudal army.

In a retour of 1642 (Inverness, 66) Macdonald of Retland is allocated one-third of Morar or ten merks.

There is a distinction between the Morar estate as a legal entity and South Morar as a geographical district.

Map 8

occupying the lands of Morar without a title. It has been suggested that North Morar was the first estate of Ranald's second son Donald, who is regarded as the founder of the Glengarry branch. Donald died in 1420 and it wasn't until the time of his son Alasdair na Coille that the family actually acquired Glengarry. During the fifteenth century there was a less rigid distinction between the Clanranald and Glengarry branches. They were all Ranaldsons – and referred to as such.

It may be that at the time of the original charter of 1498 North Morar was not necessarily regarded as belonging to a separate family of Glengarry. The distinction between the two families was in process and not yet complete. The three North Morar farms retained by the South Morar estate represent the north-western tip of North Morar and included what is now Mallaig. Today the harbour is a strategic ferry terminal. We know it was a ferry-crossing to Knoydart during the eighteenth century. Perhaps the bay enjoyed a similar function in preceding centuries. In this case the main Clanranald family may have decided to retain this particular corner of North Morar rather than let it devolve to a cadet family. Over the next century the two branches of Clanranald drifted apart and the divergence of lineage became reflected in the ownership pattern. The fact that the names continue in the later listings of the South Morar estate may simply be because the clerks copied details that were no longer relevant. It would not be the first time in Highland history that the written records credit a family with owning land they did not physically possess.

Arisaig

Arisaig was the most important district in the area. It was a 30 pence or 30 merk land and included the parish church. In the Register of Paisley Abbey there is a later copy of a charter dated September 1250 which lists, as a witness, *'Elia persona de Arasech'* (Elia, parson of Arisaig). The reference is important for its context rather than its content. The matter pertains to Paisley Abbey, mainland Argyll and its bishop. The Macruari-sponsored parson of Arisaig is involved with the ecclesiastical affairs of Scotland, despite the Norwegian leanings of the Macruaris and Norwegian ownership of the Hebrides.

Moreover, whereas North Morar was a poor and distant appendage to the Glengarry chiefs, there is circumstantial evidence that Arisaig was a central and favoured part of the Clanranald estate. There are stories that the chief's family summered here, and certainly there is

more cultivable land at Keppoch and Ardnafuaran than on the rocky
shores around Castle Tioram in Moidart. There are accounts of them
shooting seals off the rocks in Loch nan Ceall and *c.* 1588 Allan Og,
heir to Clanranald, was murdered by his brothers when so engaged.
This affinity with Arisaig continued into the nineteenth century when
Clanranald built his mansion by Loch nan Eala, close to the crannog
which may have been his ancestors' residence in mediaeval times.

There is also evidence that Arisaig enjoyed a brief spell of cultural
prominence in the middle of the sixteenth century. This takes three
forms: a map in London, grave-sculpture in Kilmory, and the records
of Henry VIII.

The Cartographic Evidence

About 1565 an English antiquarian named Laurence Nowell drew a
map of Scotland for his patron William Cecil, councillor of Elizabeth
I and one of the most powerful men in England. Strictly speaking,
Nowell drew two maps. One was at a larger scale and spread over
four pages in black ink. The smaller-scale map is in two sheets, also
in black but with the names of the principal landowners overwritten
in red. In *The Early Maps of Scotland* D G Moir comments on the
'surprising degree of accuracy' in the Nowell maps:

> The Nowell map in its latitudes and longitudes is in fact more
> accurate than Mercator's map of 1595 or Blaeu's map of 1654 ...
> Not until Dorret's map of 1750 was more overall accuracy shown
> in the shape of Scotland.

On the larger-scale version of the map we find the name 'Arsick',
or Arisaig, which is only slightly out of place, being marked at the
head of Loch Ailort (see Plate 4). There are very few settlements
marked on the west coast of Scotland and 'Arsick' is one of them,
apparently considered as worthy of inclusion as Dunstaffnage Castle
or the site of Saddell Abbey. Now whilst this prominence may be
perfectly understandable to the residents of Arisaig, for the rest of us
it requires some explanation. Why was it that a tiny settlement on
the north-west coast of Scotland, a settlement which had no castle,
and in which the church was probably the only stone building, should
be marked on a map drawn for one of the most powerful families in
England?

The mystery deepens when we consider that most of our earliest, detailed, maps of the west coast of Scotland are those produced by J Blaeu for his Atlas of 1654. In turn, most of these are attributed to Timothy Pont, Minister of Dunnet in Caithness, who did his surveying in the period 1590–1610. Pont's work was on a monumental and unprecedented scale and he can certainly be regarded as the father of Scottish cartography. Nevertheless Blaeu's map of Braid-Allaban, Lochaber etc., is geographically very weak for the area between Ardnamurchan and Glenelg. It is based on maps made by Robert Gordon who, whilst he had access to Pont's notes and sketches, seems to have lacked a draft map such as Pont prepared for other areas.

If we compare early outlines of the west coast, and the place-names given, we can trace the ancestry of the various maps that survive (see Maps 9, 10 and 11). Those in Group A derive from Laurence Nowell's map of c. 1565, those in Group B from Gerard Mercator's map of 1564. The outline followed by Group A is remarkably accurate and the sea-lochs between Loch Hourn and Loch Ailort are correct in number, order and name. In 1594 Gerard Mercator died and the 1595 map published by his son, Rumold, abandoned the outline he had used in 1564 in favour of that adopted by Group A. Presumably the Mercators had come to the conclusion that it was more accurate.

Group C is represented by a single map, that of Nicolas Nicolay, eventually published in 1583. In 1546–7 Nicolas had obtained a rutter or book of sailing directions from the Lord High Admiral of England. The rutter was the work of Alexander Lindsay, pilot for James V's voyage to the Western Isles in 1540. With the book was a sea-chart, 'rather roughly made'. However, Lindsay's rutter contains little information about our area whilst the chart has a rather different outline of the west coast. The section between Loch Nevis and Loch nan Uamh is not as accurate as Nowell, nor is there a settlement marked at Arisaig. Nevertheless this map represents another independent source dating back to at least 1540.

The maps of Gordon, Blaeu and Jansson in Group D are the least accurate of all. However, on the basis of their place-names they can be linked to Pont's notes in Macfarlane which were quoted in Chapter 1.

Our two earliest maps are those by Nowell and Mercator. These share certain features which point to a common source. This was almost certainly a map by John Elder which is now lost.

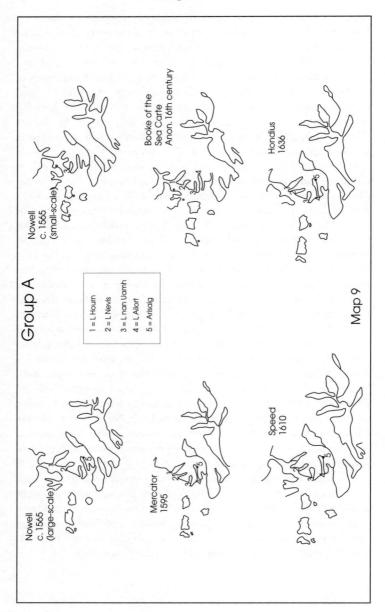

Group A

Nowell
c.1565
(small-scale)

Booke of the
Sea Carte
Anon. 16th century

Hondius
1636

Nowell
c.1565
(large-scale)

Mercator
1595

Speed
1610

1 = L Hourn
2 = L Nevis
3 = L nan Uamh
4 = L Ailort
5 = Arisaig

Map 9

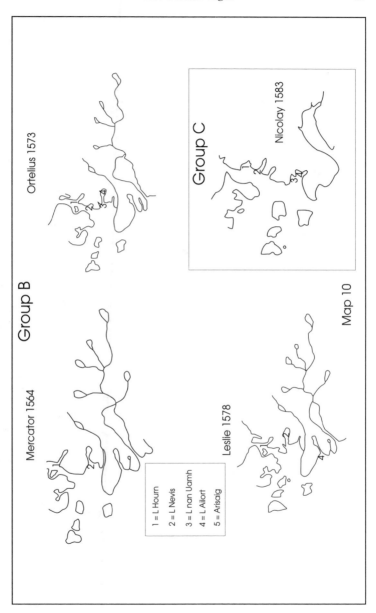

Group B

Mercator 1564

Ortelius 1573

Leslie 1578

Group C

Nicolay 1583

1 = L Hourn
2 = L Nevis
3 = L nan Uamh
4 = L Ailort
5 = Arisaig

Map 10

Group D

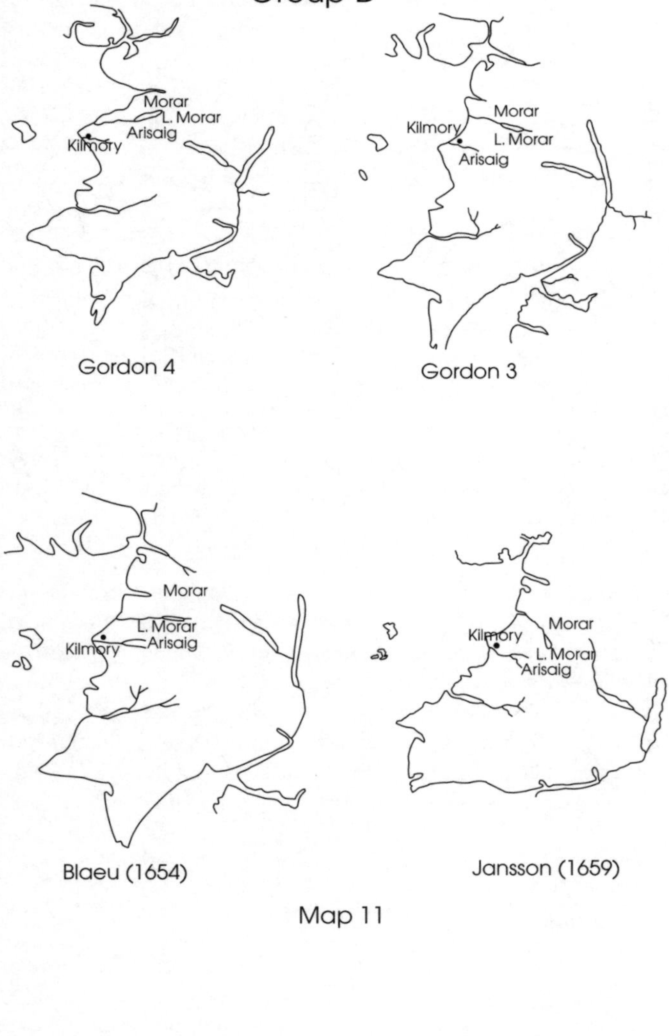

Gordon 4

Gordon 3

Blaeu (1654)

Jansson (1659)

Map 11

John Elder

We have a surviving letter from one John Elder, clerk, to Henry VIII, which is printed in *Collectanea de Rebus Albanicis*. From internal historical evidence this dates to 1543 or the first half of 1544. Elder was a fervent Protestant. He had been born in Caithness, brought up in the Western Isles and was a scholar of St Andrews, Aberdeen and Glasgow.

The period after the death of James V, in December 1542, was a time of considerable political fluidity. Henry VIII was trying to arrange a marriage between his son Edward and James's infant daughter Mary. Elder was sympathetic to Henry's cause for two reasons. Firstly he was Protestant and vehemently opposed to Cardinal Beaton. Secondly he foresaw an English alliance as favourable to the chiefs of the western clans. He twice mentions Henry's generosity to the Irish lords and plainly wanted this extended to his friends in the Hebrides. Apparently he drew a map to accompany his letter and although the map is now lost, we can use Elder's text to fill in some of the background to the maps by Nowell and Mercator.

As far as Tudor politicians and councillors were concerned, maps were important not just as geographical representations but also as projections of regional political power. Tudor civil servants were keen to know who were the important local families and where they were based. Either because he knew this fact, or because he was prompted, Elder included the names of ten 'Irish' (i.e. Gaelic) lords on his map and lists them in his letter. Eight of these lords are also marked by Nowell on his small-scale map which gives us a good idea of where he got his information from.

One of these names is particularly revealing. Elder gives it as *Mak Eoyn whanyghe* which is a corruption of MacEoin Chathanach (i.e. son of John Cathanach or John of the Battles, a chief of the Islay MacDonalds who was executed *c.* 1494). This name appears in Nowell as *Mc owin whaniugh* and in Mercator (1564) as *Mac Foyn Cannagh lord of the read Shankes*. The phrase *Lord of the Redshankes*, which Mercator employs again near Lovat's name, confirms John Elder as the source for both mapmakers. Elder's letter is full of references to redshanks, or Highlanders; indeed he regarded himself as one. The name, which means red (or tanned) legs, apparently derived from the Highland habit of 'goynge alwaies bair leggide and bair footide ...

therfor ... the tendir delicatt gentillmen of Scotland call ws Redd-
shankes.'

The coastline for our area is more accurate in Nowell than Mercator and may well represent a closer copy of Elder. Nowell was in
the employment of Cecil and had direct access to state documents.
John Elder was, by his own account, familiar with the west coast
and his evidence suggests detailed geographical knowledge amongst
the islanders:

> I was borne in Caitnes, ... educatt, and brought vp, not onely
> in the West yles ... namede Sky and the Lewis, wher I haue bene
> often tymes with my friendis, in ther longe galleis, arrywing to
> dyvers and syndrie places in Scotland, wher they had a do.

However, there are features, such as the settlements at Arisaig and
Kilmallie (by Fort William), which are peculiar to Nowell. They do
not occur in Mercator's map of 1564. Now both these sites had some
ecclesiastical significance. Elder was an ardent Reformer and possibly
not so interested in places of religious rather than political importance.
This suggests that Nowell had another source as well, one who was
knowledgeable about the church in the Highlands. Who was this
person? There is a candidate from Arisaig who was a contemporary
of, and very probably knew, John Elder. But first we must immerse
ourselves in the events of 1545.

1545

1545 was a critical year in West Highland history, arguably just as
important as 1745. It saw the last major attempt to restore the
Lordship of the Isles, an institution that had been the political focus
of the Highlands and Hebrides, formally or informally, from the days
of Somerled in the 1150s. We do not know what political institutions
the earliest Viking invaders founded in the region but from about
980–1065 the Hebrides fell under the sway of the Earldom of Orkney
before becoming part of the Kingdom of Man from 1079. After
Somerled's two rebellions in 1156 and 1158 the Southern Hebrides,
based around Islay, went to Somerled's family, whilst the Northern
Hebrides remained with the family of Man.

After the failure of Hakon's expedition in 1263 the Kingdom of
the Isles came to an end and was absorbed into Scotland by the Treaty
of Perth in 1266. In the following centuries Somerled's family gradually

extended their control northwards. In the Lordship of the Isles they created a stable political framework that endured until the end of the fifteenth century. Increasing difficulties with the Scottish kingdom meant that the Lordship was forfeited in 1475, partially restored, and then forfeited again, finally, in 1493.

The Kings of Scotland favoured the Campbells under the Earls of Argyll, and the Macdonalds saw their power continually eroded. Donald, the last Lord of the Isles, was kept a prisoner for many years, before finally escaping from Edinburgh Castle in 1543. Until his death at the end of 1545 Donald engaged in a last desperate attempt to restore the Lordship. As during the Wars of Independence the regional forces in Scottish politics played out their schemes against the larger backdrop of a national struggle between Scotland and England. The motives of the participants were diverse and complex and we need to be clear about the various interests involved in order to understand how they affected this area.

Donald Dubh, the legitimate representative of the family of the Lords of the Isles, wanted his Lordship back. He was supported by chiefs from virtually all the Western Isles except for the family of Islay under James Macdonald. He was also supported by much of the mainland west coast of Lochaber. There was a lordship to reclaim and scores to be settled with the Earls of Argyll and Huntly. This was the West Highland setting but there was also an international context.

Mary Queen of Scots was born in December 1542, just a week before her father, James V, died. Henry VIII of England wanted the infant Mary to be married to his own son (later Edward VI), and initially this was agreed in July 1543. By December of the same year this agreement was repudiated by the Scottish Parliament. Within Scotland the Earl of Arran (the heir presumptive) was Regent but there was much jockeying for position. After Arran the next in line was the Earl of Lennox.

In 1544 and 1545 the Earl of Hertford invaded Scotland in what became known as the 'Rough Wooing'. Henry VIII was determined that Mary should marry his own son and used military pressure to argue his case. Lennox was opposed to Arran and had been active against Argyll in 1544 which, of course, endeared him greatly to most West Highlanders. Thus political circumstances brought Henry VIII, Lennox and the West Highland clans together.

Some of the correspondence between the Highland chiefs and the

English authorities survives in the English records. A summary of principal events is given in Figure 3, and the following extracts from some of the more important documents give a flavour of the times.

On 5 August 1545 Donald wrote to Henry VIII:

> To your most illustrious highness, most invincible King, from our inmost heart we offer most humble submission ... we have come, therefore, most potent prince, to your Majesty's country of Ireland, attended by four thousand soldiers; ... to offer most diligent service; ... And how great is the joy I feel, reflecting in my mind how your most christian majesty, ... hath not disdained to stoop yourself to our humble condition, although from our mother's womb we were bound in the yoke and servitude of our enemies, and to this very time overwhelmed with the filth of the prison, and with intolerable fetters most cruelly bound.

In essence Donald wanted Henry's financial and military support. If he were going to take on the Earl of Argyll and the Kingdom of Scotland, he needed assistance. However, beneath the florid language is a latent threat. Donald had arrived in Ireland with 4,000 men in 180 galleys. If Henry did not feed his men, they might find other employment in Ireland that would prove a less attractive prospect.

Since Donald could not even sign his own name we must conclude that this letter, and the numerous other papers drawn up at the time, were not the work of Donald or his Council of chiefs, but instead of the two commissioners who represented them. These were Rore Ranaldson, brother to the Chief of Clanranald, and Patrick MacLean, brother of MacLean of Duart. The humble tone of the submission to Henry VIII invites parallels with John Elder's petition a year or two earlier. There is no evidence to connect them but we know that Elder was familiar with the Western Isles chiefs, in particular the MacLeods, and the MacLeods were active supporters of Donald Dubh. Perhaps the most striking difference between Rore and John is their attitude to bishops. John had little good to say of them whilst Rore wanted to become one.

The Irish Privy Council were concerned to placate the Hebrideans, in case they caused havoc in Ireland, and bought them off with £500 and provisions, whilst awaiting Henry's instructions. Rore and Patrick were in Dublin on 13 August but by 23 August were with Henry in England where they proposed certain Articles of Agreement. After input from Lennox these were slightly modified at the beginning of

The Events of 1545

February 1545	Invasion by Donald Dubh anticipated in Ireland
June 1545	Donald Dubh offering to serve Henry VIII
28 July 1545	Commission to Rore Ranaldson and Patrick MacLean to treat with Henry VIII
5 August 1545	Letter from Donald Dubh to Henry VIII
23 August 1545	Articles proposed by Rore Ranaldson and Patrick MacLean
4 September 1545	Revised articles agreed between Henry and Highlanders
5 September 1545	Henry's Council makes arrangements to send Irish troops
5-7 September 1545	Rore Ranaldson returns to Ireland from England
15 February 1546	Rore Ranaldson and Patrick MacLean detained in Dublin
13 May 1546	Rore and Patrick still detained in Dublin. Write to Henry requesting release
September 1546	Rore and Patrick still in Dublin - should be given some reward and despatched
November 1546	Warrant for £80 to Rore and Patrick
14 April 1547	A respite (Register of the Privy Seal) to Rore Ranaldson for his 'tresonable passing in Ingland' etc.

(This table is based on contemporary official records)

Figure 3

September. The substance of the final agreement was that: Donald, Lord of the Isles, would support Lennox's army in the field; with 8000 men if he moved against the Earls Huntly and Argyll, 6000 men if he moved against Dumbarton or the west of Scotland. That Donald's supporters were to be included in any agreement with the Scots. That Henry would pay the wages of 3000 of Donald's men for two months, at the same rates as his own. That Henry would give Donald a pension.

The two commissioners were sent back to Ireland and Henry made arrangements to raise 2000 Irish troops. And then at the critical moment, there was division and delay. English gold is supposed to have been inequitably dispersed. Many Hebrideans returned home. Lennox did not sail from Ireland until mid-November and achieved little. Donald Dubh took a fever and died at Drogheda.

James Macdonald of Islay was nominated as his successor but did not command the same degree of support among the island chiefs. After briefly flirting with the idea of reviving an English alliance, James abandoned any attempt to reclaim the Lordship. This was the last instance of concerted action by the islanders to resuscitate a structure that had been their political focus for hundreds of years.

What comes out of the correspondence is the welter of interests and fears at play. The Highlanders were bitterly distrustful of Scotland and wary of a separate agreement between Henry and the Scots that would leave them exposed. (They were right to be so cautious. Lochiel, who had, by his own admission, taken a prey or two from both Huntly and Argyll, was captured and beheaded.)

John of Moidart needed safeguards in case his slaughter of the Lovats at Blar Leny had consequences. Rore Ranaldson wanted to be Bishop of the Isles and wanted Henry to help him. The Highland chiefs wanted revenge on Argyll and Huntly and the Lowland government. They wanted their ancient rights restored and the usurpers punished. Henry VIII wanted to bully Scotland into marrying Mary to his son Edward. He also wanted to send the most savage Irish to Scotland in the hope of disposing of them. The Irish Privy Council wanted to be rid of the Scots whom they regarded as a menace.

The failure of the rising meant that Edinburgh's policy of divide and rule would continue to work. It was the last time the Lordship chiefs acted as a unit. Within fifty years the Macleans and the Macdonalds were at each others' throats. But although the Highland chiefs were constrained to accept the new order, they continued to feel politically and culturally alienated. In terms of a political settlement the Highland problem would endure until 1746.

Kilmory, Arisaig

But what has all this to do with Arisaig? Well, Rore Ranaldson, bishop-elect of the Isles, was priest of Kilmory, Arisaig, and brother of the most famous and powerful chief of Clanranald – John of Moidart. Rore himself had a position of considerable ecclesiastical influence. At various times he held the parsonages of Kilmory (Arisaig), Kilchoan (Ardnamurchan), Kilchoan (Knoydart), Eilean Fhianain (Moidart), and became Dean of Morvern. He was probably the author of many of the documents connected with the 1545 rising and visited the court of Henry VIII of England. He was literate, cultured, wealthy and well-travelled. Like other important clergymen, he was also a patron of the arts.

In the churchyard of Kilmory are a number of carved stones. There is nothing unusual in this: there are dozens of such churchyards up and down the west coast. But there is one particular group of carvings in Arisaig that is exceptional. It drew attention as early as 1700 when Bishop Nicolson visited the area:

> Kilmarui, i.e. the Cell or Church of St Malrubber, is close to Keppoch in Arisaig. In this chapel there are several tombs of a hard bluish stone, on which there are some ancient figures very well carved, but without inscription for the most part. One would not have thought that the people of these countries had as much skill in sculpture as these tombs show them to have had. There are some on which a priest, wearing the ancient form of chasuble, is engraved; others have only figures of arms, such as large swords, or else figures of birds and other animals ... the Highlanders think with considerable probability that after the decadence of religion, when the Abbey [Iona] had been profaned and ruined, the chiefs each brought back to the churches on their own lands some of the tombs of their fore-fathers.
>
> Blundell, *Catholic Highlands of Scotland*, 1917

The following is a list of what has survived from the mediaeval period:

1. The bottom half of a slab which consists of a thick band of

interlace only. This is probably fifteenth- or sixteenth-century and in the absence of any further detail we can say nothing more about it (see Plate 9D).

2. Three slabs which now stand upright at the end of the old church. The stones are very worn but the motifs include foliated crosses, swords and interlaced foliage. One stone has a large hunting-scene. On the basis of the swords, which look to be claymores rather than single-handers, the stones are likely to date from the early sixteenth century (see Plates 9A and B).

3. A slate slab of an ecclesiastic dressed in chasuble, dalmatic and alb and holding a chalice. He is also wearing an extraordinary hat which is not a bishop's mitre. The carving is of a higher standard than anything else in Kilmory. Parts of the canopy are reminiscent of a Macdougall slab at Ardchattan which is dated 1502 (see Plate 5).

4. A badly-damaged slate grave-slab where the design of a hunts-man's hat has plainly been copied from the clergyman just de-scribed. The stone also features a claymore or two-handed sword and so can be dated to the sixteenth century. The huntsman carries a bow, and above him a dog, which is on a lead, pursues a stag and hind. There is what may be an almost completely eroded inscription (see Plate 6).

5. A cement matrix in which have been set a number of carved fragments. These include the trunk of an archer in slate, a hunting scene, and a skeletal figure which is reminiscent of the same Macdougall slab in Ardchattan where a toad is eating a corpse's entrails (see Plates 7 and 9C).

6. A Clanranald armorial panel dated 1641. Similar panels are found in Eigg and Uist. The Arisaig panel is set into a wall-tomb (as it is in Eigg). However, in each case the wall-tomb is likely to predate the panel by about a century. So either the wall-tombs were not completed or they fell into disuse and were appropriated later. A particularly interesting feature of each panel is the galley since these demonstrate a change in galley design that seems to have taken place after about 1550 (see Plate 8).

At the end of the church is an annexe in which is found a semi-circular wall-tomb. Wall-tombs are rare in West Highland churches and seem to date to after 1500. Other examples are found at Iona,

Oronsay, Eigg, Rodel (Harris) and Kilmore (Lorn). Kilmory church is undated but probably sixteenth century. There may well have been an earlier church on the same site, dating perhaps to the thirteenth century when the Macruaris established a parish here. The annexe, the wall-tomb and the sculpture suggest the new church was a relatively ambitious project by West Highland standards. So who built it?

Traditionally the founding of the church is associated with Ewen Allanson, a celebrated Cameron chief of the period. The story goes that he roasted a black cat alive and in expiation of his sins planted seven churches, one of which was Kilmory. Although this reveals a darker side to Highland folklore, it is extremely unlikely that a Cameron chief was responsible for building a church in Clanranald country.

Instead it seems reasonable to suppose that Rore oversaw a period of expansion in Arisaig. He was brother to John of Moidart, a chief who was exceptionally powerful, capable and long-lived. John was in a position to patronise his brother's project and protect his invest-ment. John also owned the island of Eigg where the church of Kildonnan houses another wall-tomb. In addition Rore may have had money to spend from Henry VIII (see Figure 3).

Rore was a literate man, as can be seen from the flowery letter he and Patrick Maclean composed to Henry VIII. He had been well educated and was familiar with the historic role of the church as patron of the arts. In the West Highlands this meant stone-carving in particular. Rore must have been familiar with the sculpture at Ardchattan Priory because it is there that we find his own tombstone. He had presumably commissioned this during his lifetime (as many did), because the space for the year of his death is left blank.

In 1500 a stone cross had been erected at Ardchattan Priory by John O'Brolchan, one of the famous family of masons who had been responsible for so much of the fine mediaeval stonework at Iona. There is no doubt that Rore would have known of this family, and it is not unreasonable to suppose he could have invited one of them to Arisaig in order to execute a commission. This may be the reason for similarities between some of the stones at Kilmory and those at Ardchattan. Let us return to the stones at Kilmory, and particularly to Numbers 3, 4, and 5 above.

We are fortunate that earlier visitors left sketches and rubbings of what they found in Kilmory because since then the stones have deteriorated badly. In 1884 H W Lumsden made a sketch which shows that the ecclesiastic (No 3) occupied a panel beside a crucifixion scene. In 1911 this is confirmed by O Blundell who left a rubbing showing the same two figures. They are also illustrated in M E M Donaldson's book, *Wanderings in the Western Highlands and Islands*, which was published in 1927 (see Figure 4). Unfortunately since then the crucifixion scene has entirely disappeared whilst the carving of the archer has deteriorated badly in the last twenty years. This is partly because the carvings are slate, which doesn't weather as well as some types of stone, partly because they have lain flat in the old church, exposed to the elements and the feet of casual visitors.

On the basis of these earlier sketches, it seems likely that we are dealing with a sort of sculptural triptych where two figures flanked the crucifixion scene. The most likely setting for these panels is within the semicircular wall-tomb in the annexe to the church. There is ample space within this, and I give a possible reconstruction in Figure 5 where I have included the archer and the skeletal figure. Again we find a parallel with the Macdougall slab at Ardchattan where six canopied figures are arranged within two triptychs. It is possible that in Arisaig there were other panels above or below, as in the Macleod monument at Rodel in Harris, but the main feature must have been the triptych.

Moreover, because it is made of the same type of stone and is similar in its treatment of clothing, the kilted archer may have been the third or leftmost panel. This has suffered badly in the recent past but from earlier photographs we can reconstruct his figure. Part of his bow has been detached and placed upside-down elsewhere in the matrix. The only puzzling aspect is that he is pointing his bow to the left, which would give an asymmetric and unbalanced tone to the overall design. However, it would have been unacceptable for him to be pointing the arrow *towards* the figure of Christ, so perhaps we should accept this idiosyncrasy for what it is. Lumsden's sketch suggests that the archer also carried a chalice.

So who are the figures supposed to represent? The ecclesiastic is not wearing a mitre but a most extraordinary hat which M E M Donaldson suggested was a copataine. These are on record from the early sixteenth century and were worn by ecclesiastics. As Rore Ranaldson was Bishop-Elect for the Isles and had been present at the court of Henry VIII, it seems reasonable to ascribe this exotic headgear to him. The archer is then likely to be his brother, John Moidartach,

Mediaeval sculpture from Kilmory, Arisaig

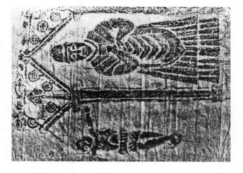

C) Blundell 1911

B) Bonus 1927

Figure 4

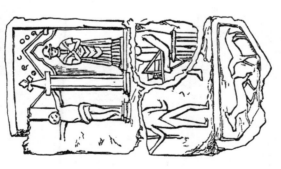

A) Lumsden 1884

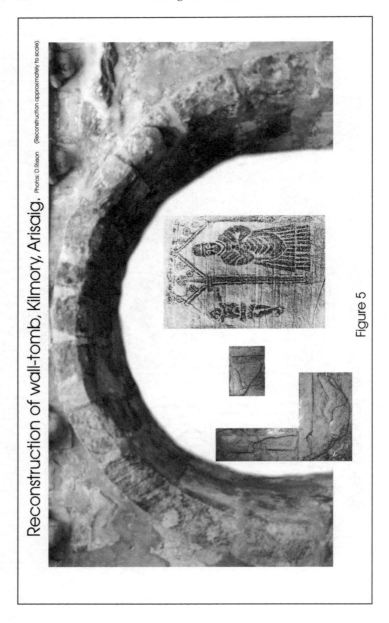

Reconstruction of wall-tomb, Kilmory, Arisaig. Photos: D.Rixon (Reconstruction approximately to scale).

Figure 5

very much a warrior-chief. In 1544 John had, by his own admission to Henry VIII, been responsible for the slaughter of Lord Lovat and 260 Frasers at the Battle of Blar Leny.

Bishop Nicolson was surprised at the quality of sculpture he saw in Arisaig and assumed, as many have done since, that the stones actually came from Iona. Instead it seems likely that, as at Rodel, a master-craftsman was brought out to work in the parish church of a Highland magnate. The Bishop's reference to birds is tantalising and raises the possibility that some of the mediaeval carvings remain hidden. In his article Blundell illustrates a fragment which is not presently visible.

Whoever executed these panels started something of a local fashion because the huntsman's hat in No 4, instead of being the hood with liripipe as at Kilmory, Knapdale, or the neat caps at Rodel, Harris, is plainly a copy of the clergyman's hat in the triptych. This huntsman also carries a bow and holds his dog by a lead. There are in fact only four representations of archery in nearly 700 carved slabs and crosses in the West Highland series. Two of these are in Arisaig, a third is on a sixteenth-century slab in Kilchoan, Knoydart (of which Rore was also vicar), and the final example is the quiver at Rodel in Harris. Bows and arrows were an important part of the West Highland armoury and survived longer here than in other parts of Britain. It is pleasing to find the best confirmation of this in Arisaig.

It seems we have a golden moment for Arisaig. A famous warrior chief and his cultured brother rebuilt the local church and adorned it with fine sculpture. At the same time a man whom they probably knew, John Elder, was making the first really accurate map of the west coast of Scotland. Somehow Rore, who visited both Dublin and the English court, was the conduit for additional information about sites of ecclesiastical importance in the Highlands. Elder probably noted Castle Tioram and Inverlochy, power-bases of Clan Ranald and Clan Cameron respectively. Arisaig and Kilmallie, which were the relevant church sites, may have held no interest for him. Yet they were eventually transmitted to Nowell, and Rore Ranaldson, parson of Kilmory, is a likely source. He, quite literally, put Arisaig on the map.

This does not seem so far-fetched if we look at it from the English point of view. The Cecil family was careful to collect political information that was relevant to Elizabethan policy. William Cecil used Laurence Nowell, one of the most gifted Elizabethan antiquaries, to do this in both a Scottish and Irish context. Nowell had access to the English state papers, including presumably Elder's map. He also visited Dublin briefly in 1560. Who knows what information Rore conveyed to the English authorities, either on his trip to England or during his enforced sojourn in Dublin?

Elder and Nowell not only drew the physical features of Scotland but added crucial facts about ownership. The coastline is astonishingly accurate but, not surprisingly, some of the locational information became confused by the time it was redrawn by Nowell *c.* 1565. Arisaig is slightly out of place and the chief's name Eoin McKalline (John of Moidart?) is too far north. Nevertheless Arisaig would have meant something to the Cecils. It was the locus of this important, literate, cleric who happened to be the brother of a powerful chief who had successfully defied the Scottish government for years. Arisaig was probably better known in 1565 than it was for another two centuries.

CHAPTER 4

THE 'FORTY-FIVE:
SOURCES AND NARRATIVE

'Jacobite' is the name used to describe a supporter of the family of King James VII (Latin, Jacobus = James) who lost the throne of Britain in 1688. For the next three generations the Jacobites plotted and intrigued to win back the crown, first from James's daughters, Mary and Anne, then from the Hanoverians. There were three main attempts – in 1714, 1719 and 1745 – all of which failed. In military terms much of the Jacobite strength came from Highland clans like the Macdonalds. By 1745 there had already been two failures and the fundamental conditions had not changed. For there to be any chance of success there had to be substantial foreign support in the form of men, money and arms.

In the autumn of 1745 Bonnie Prince Charlie arrived off the west coast of Scotland with none of these. He was indeed an adventurer and opportunist. He was ambitious to win back the throne for his father and the air was full of promises. Some Highland chiefs supported him, others declined or were actively opposed. In the event his campaign met with unexpected early success. He defeated the government forces at Prestonpans and marched as far south as Derby without raising the English support he expected. There was then a long retreat northwards before final defeat at Culloden in April 1746. For the next six months Prince Charles was hunted throughout the West Highlands and Islands. Despite a huge reward on his head he evaded capture and eventually escaped to France in September 1746. The whole campaign passed into myth and has spawned countless books, many of them containing a great deal of romantic claptrap. In the cold light of day the '45 Rising had disastrous consequences for parts of the Highlands, and it is important to disentangle contemporary facts from our subsequent projections.

Arisaig

If any area can claim to be the Jacobite heartland, Arisaig it is. Here it was that Bonnie Prince Charlie first landed on the mainland in July 1745. Here it was that his first supporters joined him, here he fled after Culloden, and it was from here that he eventually left for France in September 1746. His hopeless adventure has been rehearsed many times so I will confine myself to those aspects of the campaign which directly affected this area and its inhabitants.

One of the reasons we know so much about it is Robert Forbes. Forbes was an Episcopalian clergyman, later bishop, who was imprisoned as a suspected Jacobite in 1745 and who made it his task in after years to collect as many details about the Rising as he could. He was scrupulous in cross-checking witness statements, which means that whilst we must always exercise our critical judgement, we are at least dealing with someone whose primary objective was to collect all the available facts. His meticulous, almost obsessive enquiries were collated and published in the volumes of *The Lyon in Mourning*. These make for fascinating reading but are not always consistent as to date, or even content. This is perhaps not surprising given the different perspectives and experiences of the people concerned. In addition some reminiscences were undoubtedly 'modified' with the passage of time.

In a way such complications simply make the problem more intriguing. There was a range of opinions and loyalties at the time and these were affected by the personal trauma of the participants as events unfolded. Instead of a simplistic assertion of the unswerving loyalty of all Jacobites we perceive a more complex reality. As their resolve was tested in very adverse circumstances, so some were found wanting – for reasons we can well understand – whilst the reputation of others remains intact. This last loyalty, the blind fidelity of men in the Borrodale and Glenaladale families, whatever the personal cost, is what later writers have found so attractive.

Nevertheless we must recognise that our accounts are primarily concerned with the upper layers of Highland society. The poor and landless had little choice about their involvement in a campaign which brought them unmitigated disaster. There is evidence that not everybody felt ecstatic about enlistment and that in the aftermath there was resentment of the chiefs and factors. For a chief or tacksman to

lose his cattle was a financial disaster, for someone at the bottom of
the economic and social scale it meant starvation.

Highland society in 1745 was fundamentally hierarchical. The poor
had no voice and they have been given little voice in any history since.
Because of his social status John Mackinnon, one of the Prince's
helpers in the following narrative, was not physically harmed by his
redcoat captors. On the other hand, John McGuines, one of his
common followers, was whipped with the cat o' nine tails 'till the
blood gushed out at both his sides'.

The Events

Bonnie Prince Charlie arrived at Borrodale in Loch nan Uamh on
July 25 1745. This was Clanranald country and although Old Clanranald would not join the Prince, many of his tenants on the mainland
came to Charles's support under young Clanranald and Kinlochmoidart. His standard was raised at Glenfinnan on August 19, the
Camerons joined him and he marched away. The men from Arisaig
and Morar were enlisted in two separate regiments depending on
whose lands they tenanted. The men from North Morar belonged to
Macdonell of Glengarry and so were recruited along with the men
from Knoydart. They joined the Prince on 26/27 August at Laggan
Achdrom in the Great Glen. The men from South Morar and Arisaig
were Clanranald's and so enrolled under his son and Macdonald of
Morar. They shared a common fate but the details differed. However,
the lines of demarcation between Highland regiments may have been
relatively flexible. Several Clanranald tenants actually seem to have
served in Glengarry's regiment.

In April 1746 the Jacobite army was defeated at Culloden. Bonnie
Prince Charlie fled west via Loch Arkaig and Glen Pean to Arisaig.
From here he was taken by boat to Benbecula. He spent time in the
Outer Hebrides before returning 'over the sea to Skye' at the end of
June. In July he was brought back to North Morar by the Mackin-
nons. He travelled overland to Arisaig and was then spirited away
north and east through a tightening government cordon. He ended
up sheltering east of Fort William, in Cluny's Cage on Ben Alder,
until mid-September when he returned to Arisaig for the last time.
He left Loch nan Uamh for France in the early hours of 20 September
1746.

Retribution

In the period immediately after Culloden there was some hope amongst the Jacobites that their troops could be rallied. Large numbers of armed Highlanders were still active in Clanranald country. Arms and money were landed from two French ships, the *Mars* and *Bellone*, which arrived off Arisaig in May. Three Royal Navy frigates fought an action with the French ships in Loch nan Uamh. There were heavy casualties on both sides before the British ships withdrew. However, as time went on the full force of government made itself felt. Hanoverian troops moved west, punitive expeditions were mounted, cattle were driven away and houses burned. Militia from other parts of the Highlands were stationed at remote outposts such as Earnsaig, safe from Jacobite reprisals, but easily reinforced or evacuated by sea. Naval ships such as the *Furnace* under Captain Fergusson brought the unpleasantness of war home to the inhabitants.

In the midst of all this Bonnie Prince Charlie and other leading Jacobites lurked or 'skulked' in the area, evading capture and exposing their hosts to danger and retribution. Bonnie Prince Charlie could always escape to France; this was not an option open to many others. Only the great men could make a fresh start abroad. For the lesser gentry, their families and tenants, there was no choice but to stay and suffer the consequences.

The Sources

In order to present this story I am going to interleave some extracts from *The Lyon in Mourning* with other contemporary records. I have rearranged the accounts in chronological sequence in order to preserve the thread of the narrative. They come from a variety of sources. There is an account written jointly by Captain Alexander Macdonald (better known as the poet Alasdair MacMhaighstir Alasdair), young Clanranald and Macdonald of Glenaladale which is dated 1747. The handwriting alternates between the three contributors, so at the end of each quotation I have given the author. Alexander Macdonald was also the author of a 'Journal of the Expedition' contained in the Lockhart Papers. This gives us his own rather special perspective, neither clan chief nor common man, but poet and propagandist. There is an account written by Mr James Elphinston from journals given him by John Walkingshaw in London. Finally there is John Mackinnon's memoir of 1761 which introduces us to the most human and intriguing aspects of the whole escape saga. After Culloden the Prince is in a desperate plight. Those suspected of helping him risk losing what little the soldiers have left them. The reluctance of the chief men of Clanranald is understandable, the loyalty of men like Borrodale and Glenaladale is touching and admirable.

The first passage describes Prince Charles's welcome at Borrodale:

> We there did our best to give him a most hearty welcome to our country, the P. and all his company with a guard of about 100 men being all entertaind in the house etc. of Angus McDonald of Borradel in Arisaig in as hospitable a manner as the place could aford. H.R.H. being seated in a proper place had a full view of all our company, the whole nighbourhood without distinction of age or sex crouding in upon us to see the P. After we had all eaten plentifully and drunk chearfully, H.R.H. drunk the grace drink in English which most of us understood; when it came to my turn I presumed to distinguish myself by saying audibly in Erse (or highland language) *Deochs laint-an Reogh*; H.R.H. understanding that I had drunk the Kings health made me speak the words again in Erse and said he could drink the Kings health likewise in that language, repeating my words; and the company mentioning my skill in the highland language, H.R.H. said I should be his master for that language.
>
> Alexander Macdonald, *Journal and Memoirs*

Alexander relates how, after the battle of Falkirk, the accidental death of young Glengarry had unfortunate consequences: 'they began to desert daily upon this accident, which had a bad effect upon others also and lessend our numbers considerably.'

We have confirmation of this from a rather unlikely source. In February 1750 Mr John McAulay, Minister of South Uist, wrote two anguished letters to David Bruce, Surveyor of the Forfeited Estates. His complaint was directed at the influence of the Catholic clergymen over Clan Ranald. In particular he was aggrieved at Bishop Hugh Macdonald, brother of the Laird of Morar:

> I shall give you one Instance to Convince you how Dangerous a Man he is. In the year 1745, he was the most busy zealous promotter of the Pretenders Cause, and as he had a very great Sway among the people, It was by his Influence that young Clan,

Kinlochmoydart, and his own Brother Morar Engadged, He was like to have prevail'd with Bara and he made Attempts on Boisdale; But the Instance I am going to tell you is, When the Rebells deserted home after Falkirk, he gathered them all in one place, and made them all Swear they would never again return untill the Affair should be Concluded.

The men from Arisaig and Morar may have seen more clearly than their chiefs how the affair was bound to end.

Alexander is uncharacteristically coy about the role of the Macdonalds at the Battle of Culloden although he repeats their displeasure at being deprived of the position of honour on the right wing. He also makes repeated reference to the absence of pay during the latter stages of the campaign. Apparently this had a bad effect on morale. Perhaps the ordinary soldiers from Arisaig and Morar were looking for more than the glory of their chief. Alexander writes of the situation just before the battle of Culloden:

Our army had got no pay in money for some time past, but meal only, which the men being oblidged to sell out and convert into money, it went but a short way for their other needs, at which the poor creatures grumbled exceedingly and were suspicious that we the officers had detaind it from them. To appease them we had oblidged ourselves to give them payment of all their arrears two days before the battle, which we not being able to perform made the fellows refractory and more negligent of their duty.

Prince Charles made his escape to Arisaig immediately after the defeat at Culloden:

Upon Saturday's morning, being the 19th, he came to Oban in Kinlochmors, a corner of Clanranald's estate, and for their further security contented themselves that night for their lodgment with a small sheal house near a wood.

Early upon the 20th his royal highness got up and went straight to Arisaig to a town called Glenbiastill [Glen Beasdale], where the Prince got a sute of new Highland cloaths from Angus MacDonald of Boradale's spouse, the better to disguise him and to make him pass for one of the country. At Glenbiastill the few gentlemen (that happened to come home from that unlucky battle of Culloden) of Clanranald's men assembled about the Prince, in order to consult and lay their schemes for his present and future safety, being convinced that the enemy would probably soon be about them if not resisted. His royal highness stayed at Glenbiastill for four nights, and upon the 24th then instant his royal highness concurred in their opinions that he should leave the mainland and go to the Isles.

Captain Alexander MacDonald

The Prince was taken by boat to Benbecula and a sliver of wood from this vessel was preserved by Bishop Forbes in one of his volumes of *The Lyon in Mourning*. After some time in the Hebrides the Prince returned to the mainland with the help of the Laird of Mackinnon. The following events took place at the beginning of July although I have omitted most dates since they vary between the different accounts:

> The old Laird [of Mackinnon] and four of his men, ... ferryed his royal highness over from Skie to a place called Buarblach [Bourblach] in Glengary's lands ... Here it is to be observed, though he happened to be landed upon Glengarie's lands, that he would by no means go to Knoydart, which was very near him, nor to Lochabar, but chused to strike directly to Clan-ranald's continent to a place called Cross in Morror, from whence he was received and conveyed by Angus MacDonald of Boradale, the first house he entred in the Highlands at his first landing upon the continent.

Captain Alexander Macdonald

Prince Charles's reluctance to go to Knoydart may well have been due to the fact that many Jacobites now suspected Coll Macdonell of Barrisdale of treachery:

> ... his royal highness set sail from MacKinnon's country, ... and landed by daybreak next morning, ... at a bay in Glengary's Morror, where he stayed all that day and the following night. There are two Morors, the one belonging to Glengary and the other to Clanranald.
>
> Early in the morning ... he (the Prince) sailed into Loch-Naives, when, as he was turning at a point he was met by some of the Slate militia, who put the ordinary questions. From whence they came? Where they were bound? And they undauntedly

answering suitable to the time, the militia let them pass without taking further notice. His royal highness pursued farther into the loch, and how soon he got out of sight of them, he landed.

Young Clanranald

A more elaborate version of this incident is found in an account written by Mr James Elphinston. This gentleman had apparently been given some scrappy journals by John Walkingshaw, with the request that he put them together in a coherent, chronological manner:

The Prince and his company arrived next morning about 4 on the south side of Loch Nevis, near little Mallack, where they landed and lay three nights in the open air. The Laird and one of the men (John M'Guines) having gone the fourth day to seek a cave to lie in, the Prince, with John MacKinnon and the other 3 rowers, took to the boat, and rowed up Loch Nevis along the coast. As they turned a point they spied a boat tied to the rock, and five men with red crosses over their bonnets standing on the shore. These immediately called out, demanding whence they came. John MacKinnon's people answered, 'From Slate,' whereupon they were ordered ashore. But not complying with this summons, the five red crosses jumped into their boat, and set 4 oars agoing in pursuit of them. During the parley the Prince insisted more than once to be put on shore; but was absolutely refused by John, who told him that he commanded now, and that the only chance they had was to pull away, or if they were outrowed, to fire at the fellows, there being four fire arms on board. Upon this John, taking an oar himself, plied it so manfully, and so animated his fellow-tuggers, that they outrowed their blood-thirsty pursuers, turned quick round a point, and stood in towards the shore, which they had no sooner reached than the Prince sprung out of the boat, and attended by John and another, mounted nimbly to the top of the hill. From hence they beheld the boat with the militia returning from their fruitless pursuit, and John congratulating his young master upon his escape, asked pardon for having disobeyed him. The Prince replied that he had done well; that his reason for desiring to go ashore was, 'that he would rather fight for his life than be taken prisoner'.

James Elphinston

James Elphinston's account was given to Robert Forbes in February

1749, whereas the following passage is dated to 1761. By this time the Rising was slipping into myth and John Mackinnon has perhaps coloured his account.

Forbes writes:

Saturday, April 25th, at 11 o'clock, 1761, I was with John Mackinnon in the Infirmary of Edinburgh, when he acknowledged that John Walkinshaw of London was careless and in too great a hurry when taking down his account of things in writing, and therefore he gave me the following additions:

On turning the point they came so near to the enemy as that their oars struck upon the boat tied to the rock.

When they spied the five men with red crosses, John MacKinnon had the Prince sitting low down on the bottom of the boat betwixt his knees with his head leaning back on John's belly, and John's plaid spread over him, so that the Prince could not be seen at all. John said he was obliged to be very positive and peremptory as to keeping the Prince in his then snug situation when he offered to get up and to jump ashore, insomuch that he affirmed with an oath he would by no means allow of any such thing, as he well knew the danger of such an experiment. Meantime the Prince and John kept up a close conversation together, the Prince asking now and then how they kept their distance from the red crosses. John assured him they kept their distance very well, and that the red crosses did not gain a single foot on them.

John gave orders to the rowers to have their muskets close by them, but by no means to fire till he himself should fire first, which was to be the word of command, 'And then, my lads,' said he, 'be sure to take an aim, mark well, and there is no fear. We will be able to manage these rogues if we come to engage them.' Upon this the Prince earnestly intreated John not to take any life without any absolute necessity. John said he would observe his direction and that he would not make an attempt unless better could not be; but that if they were forced to come to blows it was necessary that none should get off to tell tidings. John observed to the Prince that as the landing place they were sailing to was all wood down to the water, they would be very safe if once there, because the red crosses would be afraid of being fired at from behind the trees or out of the thickets, and, therefore, would be sure to sheer off for their own safety. Which, accordingly, happened without their coming near to the boat in which the Prince had been.

Blaikie reported a local tradition that the Prince jumped ashore at Sron Raineach. The most likely station for the militia boat is a tidal bar of shingle just north of Earnsaig at Sgeir a' Ghaill (see Map 12). If so, it is highly unlikely they struck it with their oars but they certainly would have been much too close for comfort. After his escape the Prince crossed Loch Nevis to Knoydart, evidently to seek help or advice from old Clanranald, who was still a powerful figure in the West Highlands:

> On this eminence the Prince slept three hours, and then returning down the hill, he re-imbarked and crossed the loch to a little island about a mile from Scotus's house, where Clanranald, to whom he sent a message by John MacKinnon, then was.
>
> James Elphinston, 1749

John MacKinnon narrated to me, with no small concern, what pass'd between him and old Clanranald. When John was going to Scotus's house, he spied Clanranald at a short distance from it, who, upon seeing John coming towards him, made all the haste he could to get within doors. But John mended his pace and got hold of the tail of Clanranald's coat just as he was entring the door of Scotus's house. Clanranald turning about said, 'O! Mr. MacKinnon, is this you? I did not know you. How do you do? It is not easy to know people that come to visit us now.' 'Indeed,' said John, 'it is hard now-a-days to distinguish friends from foes. But I come as a friend, Clan, and have something to impart to you, if you will please to take a turn with me.' They went to the back of Scotus's garden, and then John told Clanranald that he came to him not only with a message but with orders to him. In some surprize and confusion Clanranald desired to know them. 'Well then, Clan,' said John, 'I am come from the Prince, who is not very far off from hence, and desires to know from you into whose hands he is now to be put, for that he will think himself safe with any person or persons you will recommend. He desires me likewise to tell you that he wants not to see you, or that you should run any personal risk on his account, as you did not join him in person, but that

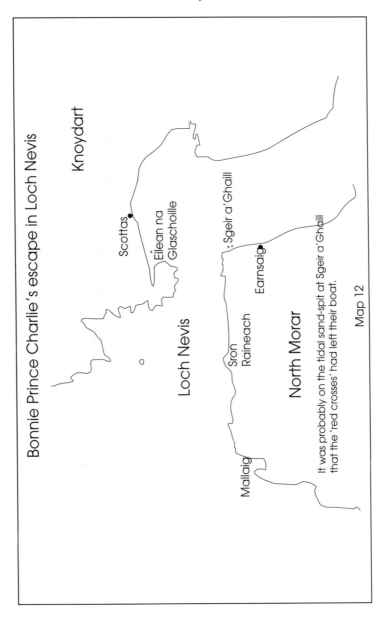

Bonnie Prince Charlie's escape in Loch Nevis

Knoydart

Scottas

Eilean na
Glascholle

Sgeir a'Ghaill

Earnsaig

Loch Nevis

Sron
Raineach

North Morar

Mallaig

It was probably on the tidal sand-spit at Sgeir a'Ghaill
that the 'red crosses' had left their boat.

Map 12

you'll only name any one with whom you think he will be safe.'
'Why,' said Clanranald, 'Old MacKinnon was with me yesterday
and did not mention a word about the Prince, or that he knew
anything at all of him.' 'In that he did right and like a wise man,'
said John, 'as he had no orders, and yet he knew as much about
him as I do, as he and I came over with the Prince from Sky.
But now I come to [you] with orders, and have faithfully delivered
them to you and wait to have your return.' 'Well then,' said
Clanranald, 'what muckle devil has brought him to this county
again? For a second destruction to it no doubt, as the troops
upon hearing of his motions, will be sure to follow him fast and
raze us all to the ground, leaving us nothing that they can either
carry off or destroy.' 'It is truly astonishing,' said John, 'to hear
a gentleman like you, Clan, talk at such a rate, when you know
the Prince to be in the utmost danger, and, therefore, that he
stands as much in need of faithful care and assistance as ever.
To whom can he go for a sanctuary in distress but to friends?
And must he not move about from place to place, as shall be
judged most fit, for to keep him out of the hands of his enemies
who are continually hunting after him? I tell you over again that
he expressly desires you may not run any risk whatsoever in your
own person, not even by looking him in the face, but that you
may name to me any person in whose hands you would judge
him to be safe. It is very hard if you will not do that much for
him in his greatest danger.' 'I tell you, Mr. MacKinnon', said
Clanranald, 'I know of no person into whose hands I can put
him. But if my advice or opinion can be of any use, it is that
you should directly return with him from whence you came and
land him speedily in the Island of Rona.' 'Indeed,' said John, 'I
would as soon give him instantly up to the troops as do any
such thing as you advise. For you know, Clan, as well as I do,
that Rona being a little grass island not a single goat or sheep
could escape a search on it, much less a man. If this be the best
advice or opinion you have to give, Clan, you had better keep
it to yourself, for the following of it would be to throw the
Prince directly into the hands of his enemies. I plainly see you
are resolved not to do the smallest service to the Prince in his
greatest distress, and that you want only to be rid of him,
therefore you shall have no more trouble about him. But remem-
ber, Sir, that I will honestly inform him of every word that has

pass'd between you and me on this subject, be the consequence what it will.'

Accordingly, John MacKinnon made a faithful report to the Prince, who received it without any emotion, and most easily said, 'Well, Mr. MacKinnon, there is no help for it. We must do the best we can for ourselves.'

John MacKinnon, 1761

Upon John's return they repassed the loch and landed at Mallack, where having refreshed themselves, and met with Old M'Kinnon and servant, they set out for M'Donald of Moran's seat, which was about 7 or 8 miles distant. As they passed a sheiling (a cottage) they spied some people coming down towards the road. Whereupon the Prince made John fold his plaid for him, and throw it over his shoulder, with his knapsack upon it, tying a handkerchief about his head, the better to disguise himself. In going along John was asked if that was his servant, to which he answered in the affirmative, adding that as the poor fellow was not well he intended to leave him at Moran's. So after receiving a draught of milk from Archibald MacDonald, son of Ranald MackDonell, son of Scotus, they pursued their journey, and came to another sheiling belonging to old Scotus, where also they bought a draught of milk and procured a guide (the night being dark and the road bad) to shew them how to take the ford near Moran's house.

James Elphinston, 1749

This ford was near Rhubana, at the sandy point where the river leaves the loch. Loch Morar has been at a higher level since the river was dammed to provide hydro-electricity:

In coming to the ford near Morar's house a comical adventure happened. Mr. MacKinnon desired the guide to be so kind as to take the poor sick young fellow (meaning the Prince) upon his back across the ford, as it was then pretty deep. 'The deel be on the back he comes,' says the guide, 'or any fellow of a servant like him. But I'll take you on my back, Sir, if you please, and carry you safely through the ford.' 'No, no, by no means,' said Mr. MacKinnon, 'if the lad must wade, I'll wade along with him and help him, lest any harm should happen to him.' Then John MacKinnon took hold of the Prince's arm and they went through the ford together. This adventure pleased Mr. MacKinnon very much, as it served to conceal the Prince more and more, for the guide had not the smallest suspicion that the sick lad was the Prince.

John Mackinnon, 1761

... and travelling the remainder of the day and the following night through hills and woods, he arrived ... in that part of Clanranald's estate called Moror, where being received by the Laird of Moror (MacDonald, of the family of Clanranald, and lieutenant-colonel of the Clanranald regiment) in a small hut, where he lived for the time, his own houses being burned by the enemy sometime before.

Young Clanranald, 1747

A little before day they arrived at Moran's borthe or hut, his house having been burned by Captain Fergusson. M'Kinnon went in alone, and Moran immediately getting out of bed, they both hasted to the door to introduce the strangers. This done, Moran's first care was to dismiss all the children and servants, keeping only his lady, who is Lochiel's daughter. She knowing the Prince at first sight, he saluted her, and the meeting was extremely tender, the lady bursting into a flood of tears. After having some refreshment of cold salmon warmed again, but no bread, the travellers left the borthe, and were conducted by Moran to a cave, where they slept ten hours, Moran being in the meantime dispatched in quest of young Clanranald. About noon Moran returned with accounts that Clanranald was not to be found.

James Elphinston, 1749

John Mackinnon's account in 1761 is more blunt:

When they came to Morar's house none could be more hearty and ready to serve the Prince, and to take all possible care of him than Morar was. But when he returned next day from seeking out young Clanranald, he became all at once very cool and backward. For when he told young Clanranald was not to be found, the Prince said, 'Well, Morar, there is no help for that, you must do the best you can yourself.' To which Morar answered, he was sorry to tell him he could do nothing at all for his Royal Highness, and as little did he know of any one to

whose care he could commit his person. 'This is very hard,' said
the Prince. 'You was very kind yesternight, Morar, and said you
could find out a hiding place proof against all the search of the
enemies forces, and now you say you can do nothing at all for
me. You can travel to no place but what I will travel to. No
eatables or drinkables can you take, but what I can take a share
along with you, and be well content with them, and even pay
handsomely for them. When Fortune smiled upon me and I had
pay to give, I then found some people ready enough to serve me,
but now that fortune frowns on me and I have no pay to give,
they forsake me in my necessity.'

This provoked John MacKinnon highly, insomuch that he told
Morar very roundly, 'I am persuaded, Morar, though you deny
it, you have met with your betters and gotten bad counsel,
otherwise you would not have changed your mind so much as
you have done in so short a time. For yesterday you was as
hearty as one could have wished to do everything for the preservation of the Prince, whose situation is just the same as when
you left us; and as there is no change at all in his circumstances,
why this sudden change in your resolutions?' Morar still persisted
in the denial of having seen young Clanranald, and of having
received any bad counsel in the matter. But old MacKinnon and
John were as positive on the contrary that he had certainly met
with young Clanranald, and that Morar's present conduct had
been the result of the conference.

This dilemma vex'd the Prince greatly, insomuch that he cried
out, 'O God Almighty! Look down upon my circumstances and
pity me; for I am in a most melancholy situation. Some of those
who joined me at first and appeared to be fast friends, now turn
their backs upon me in my greatest need, and some of those
again who refused to join me and stood at a distance are among
my best friends. For it is remarkable that those of Sir Alexander
MacDonald's following have been most faithful to me in my
distress, and contributed greatly to my preservation.' Then he
added, 'I hope, Mr. MacKinnon, you will not desert me too and
leave me in the lurch, but that you'll do all for my preservation
you can.'

Old MacKinnon, imagining these words to be spoken to him,
declared with his eyes gushing out the tears, 'I never will leave
your Royal Highness in the day of danger, but will, under God,

do all I can for you, and go with you wherever you order me.'
'O no,' said the Prince, 'that is too much for one of your advanced
years, Sir. I heartily thank you for your readiness to take care
of me as I am well satisfied of your zeal for me and my cause.
But one of your age cannot well hold out with the fatigues and
dangers I must undergo. It was to your friend John here, a stout
young man, I was addressing myself.' 'Well, then,' said John,
'with the help of God I will go through the wide world with
your Royal Highness, if you desire me.'

There is doubtless some embroidery in this account in which John
Mackinnon gives a flattering portrait of himself and the importance
of the role he played. However, it is clear that both Old and Young
Clanranald, and the Laird of Morar, were now keen to distance
themselves from the Prince.

Young Clanranald, cast in the role of villain in the above piece,
gives this account of Charles going from Morar to Borrodale:

> and having refreshed himself there that night and the next day
> as well as these troublesome times could afford, he set out the
> [next] night ..., accompanied by Captain MacKinnon and a
> guide, and arrived before day at Boradale, the place of his first
> landing, and was there received by Angus MacDonald of that
> place, who, having his houses burnt and effects destroyed by the
> troops under General Campbell's command, was obliged to
> remove with his royal highness to a hut in a neighbouring wood,
> where he refreshed him the best way he could for three days.
>
> Young Clanranald, 1747

Then the Prince proposed to go to Boradale. 'I am pretty sure,'
said he, 'honest old Aeneas MacDonald will be ready enough to
do all he can for me.' Then he asked at Morar if he would do
that much for him as to give him a guide, seeing John MacKinnon, being a stranger in that part of the country, did not know
the way thither. Morar said he had a boy, a son of his own,
who knew the road very well and whom he would send with
him as guide. The Prince very readily answered, 'If that son of
yours did never see me, well and good; he will do very well. But
if he has ever seen me, let him not come near us; we will do the
best we can for ourselves.' Morar assured the Prince his son had
never seen him, and therefore it was agreed to take him.

The Prince said he longed much to hear what they were doing in the camp at Fort Augustus, and asked if Morar could procure any one to go and bring intelligence from that quarter. Morar said there was a packman or pedlar in that corner who used to go sometimes to Fort Augustus to sell his wares in the camp, and he doubted not but he might be prevailed upon to go. The Prince pull'd out a guinea and desired Morar to give it to the pedlar to dispatch him for intelligence in Morar's own name, and to tell him to return as speedily as possible. Morar said a guinea was too much, that the one half might do very well. To which the Prince scornfully replied, 'Well, then, Sir, if you think so, give him the one half and keep the other to yourself.' After this, the Prince and John MacKinnon slipt out of the cave and went to Boradale, the foresaid boy conducting them.

John Mackinnon, 1761

So it was resolved to part with old M'Kinnon and Moran, and in the evening to set out with a boy for the house of Aneas or Angus M'Donald of Burghdale [Borrodale], in Arisaig, which was the first house the Prince was in when he came to the continent. Here they arrived before day, found the house burned by Captain Fergusson, and Mr. M'Donald himself with two men at a borthe hard by. John M'Kinnon went in abruptly, desiring that unfortunate gentleman to rise. Angus MacDonald at first was surprized, but presently knowing John's voice, he got up and went to the door, having thrown his blankets about him. Then John asked him if he had heard anything of the Prince. Aneas answered 'No.' What would you give for a sight of him? says John. Time was, returned the other, that I would have given a hearty bottle to see him safe, but since I see you I expect to hear some news of him. Well then, replies John, I have brought him here, and will commit him to your charge. I have done my duty. Do you yours. I am glad of it, said Angus, and shall not fail to take care of him. I shall lodge him so secure that all the forces in Britain shall not find him out; which he accordingly did, till he delivered him safe off his hands.

James Elphinston, 1749

After arriving at Borrodale, Prince Charles sent John Macdonald,

son of Angus, to ask Glenaladale to come and meet him 'in the
woods of Borradil':

> After Glenaladil considered the message, he looked upon it
> exceeding hard to depart from his wife and five prety weak
> children, and his great stock of catle were before then taken awy
> by the enmie; and haveing received three bad wounds at Cullod-
> den, of which one of them was not then fully cured;
> notwithstanding these consideration he despised them, and
> thought it his duty to grant all the aid and assistance in his power
> to save a poor distressed Prince.
>
>   John Macdonald of Borrodale

In the event he was no safer in Arisaig. Government ships and
troops were closing the net. There is a cave at Borrodale where he
is supposed to have sheltered. John Mackinnon, who had conducted
the Prince from Mallaig to Borrodale, was captured as soon as he
returned to Skye. He was examined on board ship by General
Campbell and soon afterwards they came to anchor in Loch nan
Uamh:

> Here John MacKinnon desired me to take particular notice that
> part of the shore towards Boradale is a rocky precipice, so steep
> that some parts of it are almost perpendicular; that in a cleft, or
> between two rocks of said precipice, there was a bothie or hut,
> so artfully contrived with the grassy side of the turf outward,
> that it exactly represented a natural green brae. In this hut the
> Prince then was, so near to the enemy that one from on board
> of any of the ships might have killed a single bird on the hut
> with a musket.
>
>   John MacKinnon to Robert Forbes, 1761

Prince Charles and his little company then sought refuge in the
hills of South Morar. Here there is another cave associated with the
Prince on the steep slopes south of Meoble. Strictly speaking it is not
a cave so much as a hole between and within some enormous fallen
rocks:

> Accordingly they pursued their journey to the Glen of Moror ...
> Upon his royal highness's arrival at his quarters, an information
> was brought that General Campbell, with six men-of-war, well
> furnished with troops, had anchored at Loch Naives (the place

where his royal highness landed from Skie in Glengary's country), whereupon two men were sent off by Loch Moror to Loch Naives to observe General Campbell's motions. But before they had time to return, Angus MacDonald ... brought intelligence that Captain Scott had come to the lower part of Arisaig from Glengary's Moror.

His royal highness and the small company that was with him, finding upon this information that Clanranald's country was surrounded on all sides by the troops, and that in all probability there could be no further security for his person in that country, it was resolved that his royal highness should leave it with the utmost dispatch ...

Glenaladale and Young Clanranald, 1747

The situation was now very dangerous and the party decided they must steal through the government cordon which was being established between the head of Loch Eil and the head of Loch Hourn. Camps were set up in a line over the hills just half a mile apart. Charles made his escape between two of these redcoat camps at dead of night and worked his way north to comparative safety:

In the course of three nights we passed by four camps and twenty-five patroles, and some so nigh us that we heard them frequently speaken, without any food farther than a smal slice of salt cheese, and aboundance of water.

John Macdonald of Borrodale

He might evade an army of redcoats, but there was one Highland resident even a Prince could not escape:

The evening being very calm and warm, we greatly suffered by mitches, a species of litle creatures troublesome and numerous in the highlands; to preserve him from such troublesome guests, we wrapt him head and feet in his plead, and covered him with long heather that naturally grew about a bit hollow ground we laid him. After leaving him in that posture, he uttered several heavy sighes and groands. We planted ourselves about the best we coud.

John Macdonald of Borrodale

In September came news that two French ships had arrived in Loch nan Uamh. The Prince was summoned and returned to

Borrodil, where he first landed; and after refreshing himself weel, directly went aboord, and with a fair wind set sail next morning for France, and left us all in a worse state than he found us.

John Macdonald of Borrodale

John Macdonald did not give voice to any sense of betrayal, he stated the facts. But beneath his comments lie a tacit criticism of this selfish adventurer with his empty promises:

He then seemed to be in good spirit, and addressed himself to such as stayed behind to live in good hopes, and that he expected to see us soon with such a force as would enable him to reembures us for our losses and trouble; so that he ended as he began.

We can only imagine the mixed emotions of those who watched the French ship slip away. On the one hand they had discharged their responsibilities. Their Prince was escaping unharmed. On the other they had to turn and face an occupying army that had ravaged the countryside and reduced an already impoverished people to misery and starvation. Any hopes of rallying the Jacobite forces must have faded quickly in the minds of locals. John Macdonald of Borrodale tells us that the gold landed by the *Mars* and *Bellone* was 'conveyed to Lochaber, and parte of the arms'. The loyal Jacobites 'were then determined to gather and randevou there friends and weelwishers, which never happened since, nor by all appearance will.'

All that the Highlanders had left was the legend and the consequences of failure.

CHAPTER 5

THE AFTERMATH

The stirring events of the campaign and the flight have cast into shadow most of the other evidence from this period. What were the military and economic consequences of failure to the West Highlands? As always, we know most about the principals, those who were literate, landed, or both. Many of these survived although Angus of Borrodale lost a son at Culloden. Government papers give us details about some of the combatants, and these are set out in Figure 6. We also learn from David Bruce's judicial rental of 22 August 1748 that a number of locals were, diplomatically, 'just now out of the country'. These were all among the more substantial tenants; the six he named held 6.5d of land between them. Such men had something to lose and so they 'skulked' in the hills whilst troops were in the neighbourhood. But these were men of substance and, in a hierarchical society like the Highlands, although the rich may have suffered, the poor always suffered more. We can only wonder at the feelings of 60-year-old Donald McGillies and his 14-year-old son as they were transported to Antigua in May 1747, and contemplated their utter loss.

This hierarchical perspective has coloured all accounts of the 'Forty-Five. In his journal Frogier de Kermadec describes a visit to Bishop Macdonald's quarters where he talked to the Bishop's sister-in-law. Macdonald of Morar's wife was a daughter of Lochiel and part of the West Highland aristocracy:

> Unable to hold back her tears she told me, while crying, that most of those I had seen seeking shelter in the mountains were nobles who, having sacrificed all their goods for their prince were now obliged to live like wretches whilst awaiting help from elsewhere.

Details of Persons from Arisaig and Morar actively involved in the 1745 Rising

No.	Name	Details	Source
1	Allan McDonald of Morar	Lt-Col, Clanranald's Regt.	Muster Roll
2	John McDonald of Guidale	Captain, Clanranald's Regt, step-brother of Allan McDonald of Morar	Muster Roll
3	John McDonald	Junior Officer, Clanranald's Regt, son of Borrodale, killed	Muster Roll
4	John McDonald	Junior Officer, Clanranald's Regt, son of Borrodale	Muster Roll
5	John McDonald	son of Allan McDonald of Morar	Muster Roll
6	Ranald McDonald	son of Borrodale	Muster Roll
7	Ranald MacDonald	son of Allan McDonald of Morar	Muster Roll
8	Bishop Hugh MacDonald of Morar	step-brother of Allan McDonald of Morar	Muster Roll
9	Andrew McInnes	Grazier, Traigh, (aged 27) Transported	Muster Roll
10	Angus MacEachen	Surgeon, Glengarry's Regt. son of Druimindaroch	Muster Roll
11	Daniel (Donald) McGillies, Arisaig	Glengarry's Regt. (aged 60),Transported	Muster Roll
12	Daniel (Donald) McGillies, Arisaig	Glengarry's Regt. (aged 14) Son of 11, Transported	Muster Roll
13	Angus McLennan, Bourblach	Glengarry's Regt. Farmer (aged 33), Transported	Muster Roll
14	Angus McLennan, Morar	Glengarry's Regt. Farmer, Transported	Muster Roll
15	Donald McLennan, Bourblach	Glengarry's Regt. Farmer, Transported	Muster Roll
16	Donald McLennan, Morar	Glengarry's Regt. Farmer	Muster Roll
17	Hugh M'Donald, Arisaig	Transported	Prisoners

1 Daniel is very likely to be an English rendering of the Gaelic name Domhnall, usually anglicised to Donald.

2 McLennan is probably supposed to be McLellan, a name with which it is easily confused. The latter is common in Morar.

3 The sources list a number of other McGillies's, McDonalds, McLellans, McLennans etc who may also have been from this area but who just appear under the general heading Inverness or Inverness-shire.

4 David Bruce's rental of 1748 reveals that Ranald McDonald (Ardnafueran), Charles McEachan (Duchamis), John MacDonald of Guidale (No. 2 above), Allan McDonald (Keppoch) and Alexander and Angus McEachen (Druimindaroch) were all either "just now from home" or "just now out of the country"!

Key: Muster Roll = *Muster Roll of Prince Charles Edward Stuart's Army*; Prisoners = *Prisoners of the '45*

Figure 6

Military Consequences

After Culloden there were still large bodies of Jacobite soldiery under arms. There was no attempt to take these on face-to-face in the Rough Bounds. The Highlanders could not be maintained for long in the field, and once they had dispersed the government could come at the individual communities as it liked. Navy ships would suddenly appear and islands like Raasay, Eigg and Canna, instead of being havens of safety, became traps that had sprung. The Hanoverians set up military outposts in the West Highlands, as for instance at Earnsaig, Loch Nevis. At first sight Earnsaig seems an unlikely base for a party of government militia. Why here, at the foot of a steep slope in an isolated corner of Loch Nevis? Why not somewhere more accessible such as Beoraid or Ardnafuaran? But our perspective is wrong. What is accessible by land was, in the context of 1746, vulnerable to surprise counter-attack. Earnsaig was not so easily reached. From here the government militia could go anywhere by boat, and escape by boat if they had to.

The French ships the *Mars* and *Bellone* arrived in Loch nan Uamh a few days after Culloden and disembarked 40,000 *louis d'ors*, plenty of arms and, apparently, some brandy. A day or two later they were engaged by three Royal Navy vessels, the *Baltimore*, *Greyhound* and *Terror*. We have accounts of the action from the diary of William Frogier de Kermadec, an ensign on board the *Mars*, and also John Macdonald of Borrodale. Frogier's account implies that the Highlanders, who had initially promised to fill the gaps in the crew of the *Mars*, did not seem keen to come back on board. There ensued a long and bloody battle before the Royal Navy boats withdrew. John Macdonald of Borrodale describes the action:

> The french frigats landed ... fourty thousand Louisdors, with some stand of arms and amunition, at the farm of Borradil; government being informed of the same, despatched three of there own frigats to the place mentioned ... The batle leasted twelve hours, and we found on our shores fefteen frenchmen dead, not one Englishman in the number, as they threew none overboard of them till they came the lenth of the point of Ardmurchan.

There is also a local tradition that one of the shore spectators was

more concerned about the effect on his goats pasturing on a neighbouring island than he was about the outcome of the battle!

John Fergusson arrived with the *Furnace* shortly after the French
had left. His report shows that the government was as determined to
prevent the revival of the Jacobite campaign as the local chiefs were
to keep their men under arms:

> next Morning being the 10th I stood into Loch Alliard [Ailort],
> and Landed my Men at Break of Day, and took possession of a
> Little Hill with 60 of them, untill the rest Search'd amongst some
> Caves, where they found 650 Stand of Arms, 2000 Weight of
> Balls, and some Flints, but no Powder, By this time the Rebells
> had gather'd into a Body of 4 or 500 Men Commanded by Young
> ClanRonald and made several Attempts on my People, who Still
> kept their ground, and drove them back with the Assistance of
> some Grape Shott, fired in amongst them. Wee got all the Arms
> etc off, and took two of the Rebells Prisoners, without any Loss,
> but one of the Tenders Men being more intent on Plunder than
> getting off, was taken Prisoner by them. My Prisoners assures
> me that the Pretender went off in an open Boat three days before
> the French Ships arrived ... The French Ships Landed a great
> Deal of Arms, Money, and Ammunition, and gave out that there
> were several more Ships on their Passage, Loaded with the same
> Cargoes, & has gott 8000 Men on board. the Cheifs I find still
> Endeavour to keep as many together of them as they can; They
> had a meeting on the 8th Instant of all the heads of them, and
> afterwards they gave out Orders for all of them to be ready to
> joyn in a Days Notice, and that they were to be joyned by some
> thousands of the French, and gett payed all their Arrears. I am
> now Cruizing off of the Isle of Rarza [Raasay] and has my Boats
> Manned and Armed ashore, burning and destroying the Lairds
> Houses with some others that belong to His Officers. I have very
> good Information where all the Arms Brandy etc is Lodged that
> came in the Last two Ships, But not having Strength enough of
> my own to attempt carrying it off I have sent an Express to
> acquaint His Royal Highness with it, for if he will Order me a
> reinforcement of 200 Men, from the Isle of Sky, I shall forfeit
> my Life if I do not Bring it all off. I shall Cruize between this
> and Loch Mudart untill I receive His Highness's Answer.

> John Fergussone of the *Furnace*, off Raasay, 12 May 1746

This incident appears briefly in his official log: 'Sent the boats on Shore and took 600 Stand of Small Arms from Loch Arsey and 25 boxs of Small Shott'.

Fergusson's policy was to discourage local resistance by direct action. He ranged up and down the coast, putting his boats ashore to search for arms and fire the houses. Highland accounts depict the activities of his troops as pretty brutal. According to John Macleod, the young laird of Raasay, Fergusson's troops went through the island, burning virtually all the houses and slaughtering much of the livestock. Quite possibly what found its way into Fergusson's log was suitably sanitised. On Sunday 18 May the entry reads:

> brought up ... in 15 fathom Water off Loch morrie [Loch Morar] ... Sent the boats on and ashore and Seat fire to the Lairds House ... brought up ... at Loch Noway in 20 fathom ... Sent the boats ashore ... [19 May] ... 84 Stand of Small Arms and 20 Barrals of Gun Powder was taken on board the Terror and Furnace from the Shore

James Elphinston confirms that Morar's house was burned by Fergusson, while John Macdonald of Borrodale states that 'our houses ... were all burned'. In 1795 Rev Alexander Campbell, Minister, wrote in the Old Statistical Account that 'Mor'ir House, which, with every hut they could discover, was burnt by the troops in 1746; who also plundered or destroyed almost all the stock of cattle, etc.'

Another consequence of military repression was the sacking of the little seminary on Eilean Ban, Loch Morar. In the *Catholic Highlands of Scotland*, Blundell has given extensive extracts from a contemporary account that was published in the *Scots Magazine*. Troops marched overland from Arisaig at the same time as naval boats were brought ashore and carried the short distance to Loch Morar. The island was then a refuge for leading Jacobites such as Macdonald of Morar and his brother Bishop Hugh, as well as Lord Lovat. To escape capture they had to abandon the seminary:

> which the sailors quickly gutted and demolished, merrily adorning themselves with the spoils of the chapel. In the scramble, a great many books and papers were tossed about and destroyed.

This took place in the summer of 1746, not long after Frogier de Kermadec had remarked of Bishop Macdonald's quarters that they contained a library of around 200 books 'as many Scottish, English, French as Greek and Latin'.

Lovat was captured shortly afterwards.

Economic Consequences

There was also the devastation caused by the government's punitive expeditions. There is no doubt that enormous numbers of livestock were driven off. In some areas, such as the Lochiel estate, we have surviving lists which show exactly what people lost. Unfortunately we have nothing quite like this for Arisaig and Morar but the evidence from Canna and Raasay suggests the losses could be grievous. Wealth consisted not in coin but in cattle, and one contemporary estimate states that more than 20,000 animals of various types were taken to Fort Augustus alone. The war had been brought home to the people of the West Highlands and the consequences for individual families could be disastrous.

The problem is that the evidence for Arisaig appears ambiguous. In 1748 David Bruce made up lists of arrears for the Clanranald estates. Although a number of tenants had paid no rent for two or three years, the proportion of arrears in Arisaig, about 47% of annual rental, is lower than on other Clanranald properties. The arrears in South Uist were a substantially greater proportion, those in Moidart twice as high, those in Canna more than four times higher. There are several possible explanations for this. Arisaig may not have suffered from as much post-Culloden devastation as other districts; or local people managed to recoup some of their losses by recently-arrived supplies from France!

An anonymous account of the Highlands, probably by David Bruce in 1750, states that the consequences of defeat were carried into the Highlands as never before:

> The People of these Wild Countries could never believe that they were Accessible 'till the King's Forces Scoured them after the Battle of Culloden which was a prodigious Surprize to the Inhabitants. The Common people, tho' Papists, Curse their Prince and Chiefs together, as they are sensible that all their Calamities are owing to them.

Fergusson's memory became notorious but it was a harsh political lesson for the area. The Highlanders were now up against a naval power, for the first time since the arrival of the Vikings 900 years earlier. Against the Scottish kings, who, apart from James V, seldom built up naval forces to use against the west, the Highlanders could always rely on distance and geography to protect them. Lowland kings were not going to waste resources chasing elusive Highlanders through the hills. But now they faced a new and unpleasant geopolitical reality. The enemy came by sea, and by sea virtually every corner of the Highlands is accessible.

This scourging must also have had an important psychological effect on locals. Throughout their previous history Highland armies had always marched off to do battle elsewhere: the Lowlands, England or Ireland. True, there were clan raids and warfare, a temporary garrison in Castle Tioram perhaps, but never before had an outside military presence been sustained throughout the Rough Bounds. The Highlanders had no shortage of fighting spirit, but waging war was now largely a matter of economic resources, a fact that must have impressed locals as they watched the naval battle in Loch nan Uamh in May 1746. No West Highland chief had a boat to match any of these.

On a lighter note we have a list of Arisaig names dated 25 January 1748. Its purpose is enigmatic but I quote some of the entries which are arranged by settlement.

Kenloidd ... [Kinloid]

Hector mcEuine – one Brandy Cask ...
Euine mcEan Oag, had one Brandy Cask stollen from him ...

Airdnafourran ...
John mcInish dep[ones] had one Brandy Cask stollen from him ...

Druimdarich ...
angus Baine mcEan vic Coile Duff Dep: lost 2 hiden Cask ...

Febr. ye 1st
Airdgasry ...
Angus McLauchl: Dep: himself half a Cask has som bottels ...

Torbay ...
Alexd McNile. the prophet depon[e]d
                    National Archives of Scotland, GD 201/1/362/5

We can have no proof but it is perfectly possible that this list refers to the cargo landed by the French ships *Mars* and *Bellone* shortly after Culloden. This apparently included spirits, and doubtless some of the local men worked to secure these against a rainy day. Whilst not perhaps their most grievous loss, the theft of these casks of brandy, presumably by Hanoverians, was certainly vexatious. We also have a story that *c.* 1810 some local peat-cutters unearthed liquor hidden at the time of the '45. Who knows what the mosses of Arisaig yet conceal; or what were the forecasts of Alexander MacNeill?

A Political Reorientation

The consequences of defeat were fundamental in that they finally altered the political and military orientation of the West Highlands. David Bruce wryly comments on the previous course of political assimilation in the region:

> The MacDonalds pretend that their Attachment to the Stuart Family proceeds from a Principle of Loyalty and Duty but it is observable of several Highland Clans, particularly the McDonalds, that they have been mostly Loyal to some King or other who was not in Possession, but seldom to any King upon the Throne, and when they could not find a Pretender they never were at a Loss for a pretence of some Kind or other for Rapine and Plunder. Their Rebellions against the State and their Depredations on the Subject on these Occasions if enumerated would fill a Large Folio, and an Octavo would hardly Contain their Rebellions against the Stuart Family whilst on the Throne.
>
> *The Highlands of Scotland in 1750*

Ever since the loss of Norse sovereignty in 1266 the Highlands and Hebrides had enjoyed an uneasy political and military relationship with Lowland Scotland. West Highland aspirations had a political focus in the shape of the Lordship of the Isles. This often led to conflict with the Lowlands, and the Lordship was finally forfeited in 1493. From then on the relationship was politically unstable. Some Highland clans, principally Clan Donald, were generally at odds with the Lowland realm. Others, such as the Campbells, made their accommodation and saw their power expand.

This is a highly generalised view of 200 years of history but the

Highland problem was as intractable in 1745 as it had been in 1545. However, in political and military terms Culloden represented a watershed. Within 30 years many Highlanders were emigrating to North America where, as often as not, they ended up fighting for the Hanoverian kings in the American War of Independence. Within two generations large numbers of Highlanders were fighting for the British Army against Napoleon.

Cultural Conflict

The relationship between the Highlands and the rest of Scotland (or Britain) has been determined by certain fundamental differences. The lines of division have been physical and cultural, and they have fluctuated over the centuries. Some of these tensions have never been resolved, but since Highlanders are now numerically weak and economically marginal they no longer represent a threat, just an uneasy reminder.

What are these lines of division? First and foremost they are geographical. The Highlands are physically different and Arisaig and Morar have always been amongst their harshest and most rugged districts. This was recognised years ago in their land-assessments and the Gaelic nickname for the area – literally the Rough Bounds. Furthermore there were divisions of language and religion, as well as economic and social distinctions. After the decline of Norse in the Hebrides the whole of north-west Scotland was Gaelic-speaking for centuries although native Gaelic-speakers are now in a minority in most areas except the Outer Isles. There were also religious differences with districts like Arisaig and Morar remaining Catholic.

As a result Highlanders had a strong sense of identity. They were culturally different to English-speaking Lowlanders. Those who spoke for the Highlanders, the poets and historians, reflected on their sense of loss and alienation. They were the original Scots. The Lowlander was the *Gall* or foreigner, who had a mortal enmity toward the Highlander.

In the mediaeval centuries the Highlanders had little contact with the English except for the purposes of military or political alliance. In more recent times the contacts have increased. The chiefly families became anglicised; many rich southerners came to the Highlands to shoot and fish. So lying on top of the long-standing hostile interface with the Lowland Scots government is a later period of interaction

with the *Sassenach* incomer. As a result the Highlander's sense of
alienation has sometimes incorporated, from the eighteenth century
onward, a nationalist or anti-English sentiment. This resonates today
in pejorative phrases like 'white settler' to describe the incomer.
Immigrants to the Highlands, like the tourists, may be sympathetic
to the culture and language that they find. The problem is that their
very presence, in an area of fragile population, is itself threatening.
It is not just a question of cultural integrity – after all every culture
continually evolves – it is rather a question of culture loss.

These lines of division found expression in centuries of political
and military conflict between Highlands and Lowlands. Over time
the Highlands as a culturally-defined area has retreated in on itself
as every border has succumbed to the economically and therefore
linguistically stronger Lowlands. It is impossible to delineate this
process exactly although critical dates would include the loss of the
Hebrides by Norway in 1266 and the loss of the Lordship of the Isles
in 1493. To these Culloden has always been added, although by itself
Culloden was not decisive. It was just another lost battle in a long
war of attrition. Even if the Highlanders had won at Culloden, even
if the Catholic Stuarts had been restored, it is unlikely that the
fundamental trends would have been reversed, any more than the
Highland clans found their fortunes revived by the restoration of
Charles II.

Over the centuries many Highland leaders, political and literary,
must have thought about this process of absorption, about the relationship between Highland and Lowland cultures. It often found
expression on the battlefield, and, in the long run, this was a war the
clans would always lose. Politically, those clans which accommodated
themselves to Lowland government emerged triumphant. But there
was also a war on a cultural front, one which sometimes expressed
itself in poetry. In a way this struggle continues: politely, quietly, but
as a deep undercurrent. Perhaps because of this, when it appears
openly and furiously, as in the poetry of Alasdair Macdonald, it
engages our interest and remains topical.

Alasdair Macdonald (Alasdair MacMhaighstir Alasdair)

Alasdair Macdonald is one of the giants of Gaelic poetry. He was
born in Moidart *c.* 1695 and died in Sandaig, Arisaig *c.* 1770. He is
buried in Kilmory where a small plaque has been erected to his

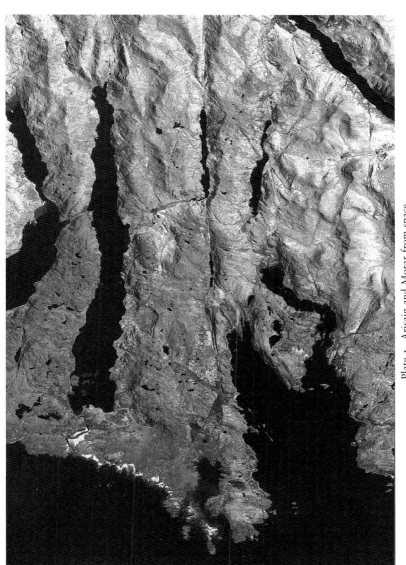

Plate 1. Arisaig and Morar from space.

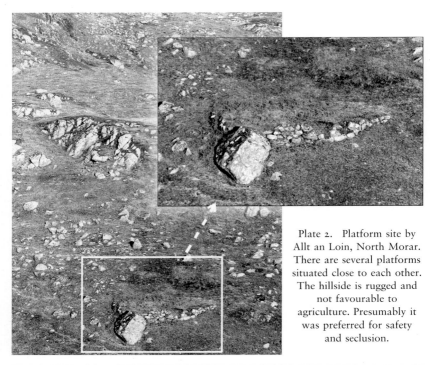

Plate 2. Platform site by Allt an Loin, North Morar. There are several platforms situated close to each other. The hillside is rugged and not favourable to agriculture. Presumably it was preferred for safety and seclusion.

Plate 3. Fertacorrie (see map 6).

Plate 4. From Laurence Nowell's map of Western Scotland, *c.* 1565.

Plate 5. Carved stone, Kilmory, Arisaig (see Figures 4 and 5).

Plate 6. Huntsman, Kilmory, Arisaig.

Plate 7. Archer, Kilmory, Arisaig.

Plate 8. Clanranald armorial panel (*above*) in wall-tomb in annexe to old church, Kilmory. Below is an enlarged view of the galley (birlinn) on the panel. There is a matching wall-tomb and panel at Kildonnan, Eigg, and a panel in Uist.

Plate 9. Mediaeval carved stones, Kilmory, Arisaig (not to scale).

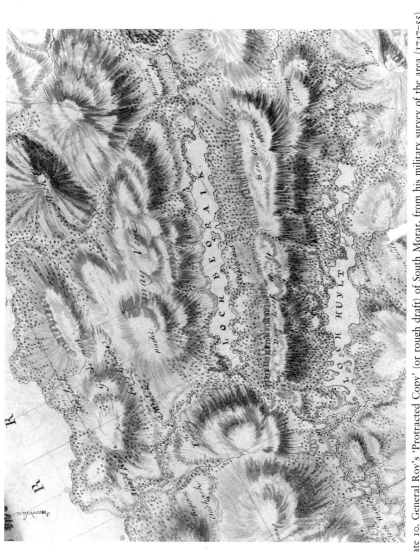

Plate 10. General Roy's 'Protracted Copy' (or rough draft) of South Morar, from his military survey of the area (1747–55).

Plate 11. Roy's 'Fair Copy' of Morar.

Plate 12. Hut bases, North Morar.

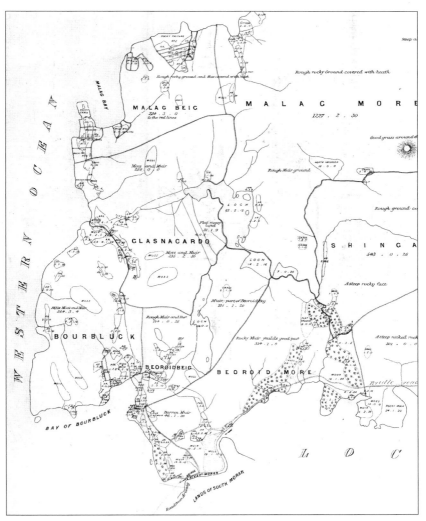

Plate 13. Boulton's map of North Morar, 1834.

Plate 14.
Farm, Loch an Nostarie, North Morar
(see map 2). This is marked as arable on
Boulton's map of 1834, but had already
fallen into disuse. The march-dyke is
visible, but was probably not built until
the late eighteenth century. The farm
itself may be much older. This is a
building against the left (north) wall.

memory. He has always attracted attention both for the quality of his poems and his larger-than-life personality. He was a fanatical Jacobite who fought for Prince Charles and became a forceful propagandist in the political and cultural struggles of his day. At various times his pen expressed frustration, rage and vitriol. In the circumstances of cultural loss we can understand his sentiments. His poetry has played a potent role then and since because it coloured, consciously or unconsciously, so many later interpretations of the period.

Much of Alasdair's poetry is 'political' in that it was inflamed with a determination to defend those things Highland which he saw threatened by Hanoverian government. He was engaged in a struggle to prevent the Highlands being overwhelmed on a cultural as well as a military front. His was by no means the only voice; a thousand nostalgic 'histories' have later elaborated the theme. Since the 1745 Rising, gallantry, song, colour and romance have been associated with the Jacobites; a dour, harsh, foreign spirit with the Hanoverians. Poetry was Alasdair's most potent weapon. His body may slumber in Kilmory, but his polemic is with us still.

Some sixty of Alasdair's poems survive, covering a wide range of subjects. His most famous work is the *Birlinn of Clan Ranald*, a long poem describing a sea-voyage in Clanranald's galley from South Uist to Carrickfergus in Ireland. His other poems fall into several categories which help define his interests and concerns. There are hymns to the Jacobites and incitements to battle. There are poems of praise for the people and causes he identified with: the exiled Stuarts, Clan Donald, Morar, Gaelic, Highland dress, bagpipes, whisky. There are biting satires on those who opposed or had offended him. This category was plentiful and included anything Hanoverian, repressive legislation, rival clans like the Campbells and the MacKenzies, even rival poets, or rather poetesses. He may well have written a lot more that has not survived. Certainly some of his pieces offended various editors down the years and have often been excluded from print. These, depending on one's perspective, could at best be described as graphic, at worst pornographic. As Rev M'Lean said in the New Statistical Account for Arisaig:

> He has been justly reprehended for the indecency of some of his productions, but it is due to his memory to state, that, for these in his latter days, he was deeply penitent.

Hmm!

Alasdair was a man of the eighteenth century when attitudes to sexuality were different. About 1735 one of his former protégés got into a scrape with the authorities for publishing *An Essay upon Improving and Adding to the Strength of Great Britain and Ireland by Fornication*. There is a suggestion that Alasdair may have produced some of his more salacious items under the patronage of a Highland 'private gentleman'.

In 1744 Alasdair co-wrote a long charge against a Mr Francis Macdonald, a Presbyterian preacher in Strontian who had formerly been a Roman Catholic priest in Moidart. Mr Francis was accused, amongst other things, of incest with his sister, and the complaint was brought by the Laird of Kinlochmoidart and Bishop Macdonald, brother of the Laird of Morar. The Presbyterian authorities were suspicious that the charges reflected spite over Mr Francis' apostasy rather than the truth. Mr Francis' sister had two children and the Presbytery let slip the allegation that Kinlochmoidart's wife suspected her own husband of fathering one of them himself! The truth of course rests forever with the good lady in question but the issue points up the keen competition locally between Catholic and Presbyterian churches. Along with the other evidence it also suggests that in the eighteenth century, Highland gentlemen were sometimes anything but.

Alasdair was a feisty, difficult character who would probably have fallen foul of the authorities in any age. He changed from Protestant to Catholic but then fell out with the local priest, Father Harrison, and was constrained to move from Moidart to Knoydart. Father Harrison had carefully avoided being caught up in Jacobitism and no doubt his moral sense was offended by portions of Alasdair's output.

Some of the themes which surface in Alasdair's poetry have run through Highland historiography from then till now. Firstly there were the consequences of military defeat. Undoubtedly there was a deeply unpleasant side to the Hanoverian victory at Culloden; undoubtedly there was harsh government repression and offensive legislation. But it is important to keep this in perspective. In less than two generations much of this was repealed, forfeited estates were returned, and the Highlands were effectively reintegrated. Highlanders became more concerned by everyday economic problems than the political allegiance of their chiefs. Alasdair's starting-point was acceptance of the hierarchical structure of the Highland world. Most people today would find this less easy to identify with than his more general defence of Gaelic culture.

There were acute divisions in the eighteenth-century Highlands. There were rivalries and resentments between the old political order, as represented by the Macdonalds, and the new, by the Campbells. There were differences between Catholics and Protestants; divisions that fell along clan lines and campaigns that were fought by SSPCK* missionaries and catechists. There were rifts between Jacobites and Hanoverians and those, like Macdonald of Boisdale and Macdonald of Sleat, who were determined not to let their people become embroiled in a perilous adventure. In this general struggle there were many more political and cultural skirmishes than there were military.

Nevertheless there are still historians who throw out wild accusations of genocide. It is certainly true that many, in both government and organisations like the SSPCK, felt less than charitable to Catholic Highlanders. The seminary on Eilean Ban, Loch Morar, was sacked by government troops and there were many attempts to convert the Catholic clans. But they resisted. In 1750 there are letters of anguish from Mr John McAulay, Minister in South Uist, bewailing his discomfiture at the hands of the Catholic population. He complained that he could not even get help from the Army officers: 'I have known some of them blame the Ministers for the trouble given them, and drunk with the Priests Instead of apprehending them'.

The State was not going to embark on a bloody campaign of conversion. This war was fought on the ground, not in the headquarters of the SSPCK or even in Rome. It was decided according to the particular circumstances of each island or mainland estate. It was determined by the allegiance of leading families and the innate conservatism of rural societies which felt themselves under threat from hostile and unsympathetic forces. Alasdair was brought up in one tradition but his sense of history and his cultural affinities threw him into the arms of another.

Cultures certainly struggle for supremacy, but to argue that there has been sustained institutional support for the suppression of the Highlands is to mistake what is fundamentally an economic issue for a political one. The Highlands in the eighteenth century were neither the time nor the place for any sort of ethnic or cultural cleansing. If we are looking for these, we are much likelier to find hard evidence

---

* Society in Scotland for Propagating Christian Knowledge.

in the campaign against the Macgregors two centuries earlier, or in the massacres of Glencoe or, worse still, Dunaverty. By the early nineteenth century the situation in the Highlands was much more amicable. When the SSPCK in Inverness conducted their surveys in 1822 and 1824, it was in order to establish where their efforts could best be directed for the issue of Bibles. The appendix to their report contains a number of letters, including several from Catholic priests, thanking them for their efforts.

One of Alasdair's concerns was the fate of the Gaelic language. Despite attempts to pin the decline of Gaelic to the Statutes of Iona in 1609 there is very good evidence locally that Gaelic was intact and healthy until the late nineteenth century. The anglicisation of the gentry is often blamed. In fact legal documents about Morar were being written in English, in Inverness, in the first half of the seventeenth century. Two hundred and fifty years later virtually every soul in Morar still spoke Gaelic. The decline in Gaelic cannot be laid at the door of the chiefs, Culloden or the Hanoverians. The real agents of change have been economic factors, the railway and the Scottish educational system.

Other concerns of Alasdair's now seem irrelevant. He defended whisky, tartan and the bagpipes against what he saw as an unsympathetic government. Today the government can only be seen as the enemy of whisky in terms of the amount of revenue it raises from its taxation, whilst both tartan and bagpipes are well subsidised in the British Army. The enemies today are more likely to be imported wine, music and clothes, all of which reflect personal choice. All Western cultures have their integrity incessantly challenged by the pull of individual freedoms.

The strength of Alasdair's poetry was perhaps also its weakness. To him the will, political will, military will, the force of words, were sufficient. His task, as bard, was to mobilise them in order to effect change. He would not have recognised economic arguments. He was still too entrenched in the past. His sympathies were with an outmoded aristocratic society where he would have a position of status. R Black quotes a letter which Alasdair wrote to Sir Alexander Murray of Stanhope, the owner of Ardnamurchan and Sunart, in December 1730: 'Amongst other favours I hope your honour will influence upon Ardshliginish to grant me at least two pennyes of Killmorry'.

Alasdair is here referring to the farm of Kilmory on the north side of the Ardnamurchan peninsula. This plea gives us an insight into

Alasdair's view of his own social standing. Though Ardnamurchan was a more valuable estate than Arisaig, a farm of 2*d* was still a significant holding. Such a tenancy would have meant he was a person of rank. In Arisaig only five people had tenancies of more than a pennyland in 1748.

He was a creature of the old Highland order and unaware of the struggle about to be played out as the Highlands were accommodated to the demands of capitalist Britain. If Gaelic culture was to survive, then it depended on political independence and economic self-sufficiency. The former was now a lost cause, the latter was always its Achilles heel. Within a year of Alasdair's death, Glenaladale wrote that his plans for emigration had driven all thoughts of the 'Pretender' from old Borrodale's head. How would Alasdair have coped with a situation where sheep and his own chief posed more of a threat to traditional Gaelic society than any number of redcoats?

CHAPTER 6

THE EIGHTEENTH CENTURY: ECONOMIC AND SOCIAL LIFE

We have very little evidence for economic and social conditions in Arisaig and Morar before 1699. However, in a conservative rural economy there were aspects of life which had probably seen little change for centuries. When eighteenth-century commentators draw attention to the poverty and what they regarded as primitive agricultural practice, it is reasonable to assume that what they described had existed for a long time.

Sources

During the eighteenth century, and particularly after the 'Forty-Five, there is an explosion of evidence as Arisaig and Morar come into enforced contact with the rest of Britain. We have the details of Bishop Nicolson's report in 1700. We have four Arisaig rentals from 1699 to 1798 and one for North Morar dated 1762. We have the reports of Jacobites and visitors like the Frenchman Frogier de Kermadec who give us little cameos. We have the maps made by General Roy's surveyors about 1755. We have the copious evidence of the Forfeited Estates papers in Lochiel, Knoydart and Kinlochmoidart. We have population estimates made by a number of observers from 1755 onwards. Even when some of these reports are from outwith our immediate area, the districts are so similar in geographical and cultural terms that we can draw meaningful analogies.

From the latter part of the century we have some estate records and evidence from the early emigrants. We have the Old Statistical Accounts for Glenelg, written by Rev Colin Maciver in 1793, and for Ardnamurchan, written by Rev Alexander Campbell in 1795. We have a rental of 1798 and last, but by no means least, we have visual evidence on the ground. Anyone who does any field-walking locally is immediately struck by the remains of a previous agricultural system. It is clear from the nineteenth-century evidence that dramatic changes had taken place well before the first full census listing in 1841. Much marginal land had already been abandoned. Rural society had already undergone a good deal of restructuring.

The Pattern of Landholding in Arisaig

We are fortunate to be able to compare four Arisaig rentals between 1699 and 1798 (see Figure 7). These confirm evidence from other districts that rents rose rapidly in the second half of the eighteenth century. This process transformed the old relationships between chief and clansman and caused major social disruption. The traditional agricultural base could not sustain the increased levels of rent. Either new forms of income had to be found, or the land had to be given up. Sheep-farmers started to occupy the Highland glens. The rental for 1748 shows us the old pattern of landholding just before it collapsed.

David Bruce travelled throughout the Highlands in the years after Culloden. Despite his work as a government agent and despite his antipathy to the chiefs, he was not unsympathetic to ordinary Highlanders. Unfortunately, probably because of their ardent Jacobite sympathies, this did not extend to the people of Arisaig and Morar:

The Remaining part of the Estate of Clanronald lys, in the

Figure 7. Rentals in Arisaig, 1699–1798					
Lands	Value (d)	1699 (m)	1718 (m)	1748 (m)	1798 (m)
Dubhchamus & Torbae	3	221	220	223	360
Sandaig	1	57	55	50	216
Ghaoideil	2	100	100	96	252
Druimindarroch & Druimnachoilich	4	283	305	296	299
Borrodale & Beasdale	5	200	200	366	614
Kinloid	2	131	135	141	454
Keppoch & Ardgasery	6	320	330	347	2633
Arieniskill	1	125	130	132	540
Polnish	1	110	110	109	756

This table includes only those farms where we can compare like-for-like and where the figures are robust. It is striking that rents barely changed over the half-century between 1699 and 1748, and then, in every case except Druimindarroch, rose dramatically by 1798. This forms the background to emigration.

Figures are in Scots merks (1=13s 4d) and are rounded to the nearest merk. They should be treated as approximate since they include converted casualties but not the King's Cess, Minister's stipend etc. A merk is two-thirds of a Scots pound. To convert £ Scots to sterling, divide by twelve. Land values are in terms of pennylands.

Countrys of Arrisaig and Moidoirt, on the Continent The Inhabitants of which ... are all Popish, and much more Uncivilized,
and more barbarous in their Natures, than the people of the
Islands.

In the course of his duties Bruce drew up a judicial rental for Arisaig
in 1748. The government was determined that none of the rebel chiefs
should be able to conceal their assets as they were thought to
have done after previous risings. All tenants had to make a sworn
deposition before Bruce. They were questioned about the size of their
holding, level of rent, state of arrears etc. The resulting document is
invaluable evidence of society in Arisaig and Morar before the break-
up of the clan system. The land was divided into settlement units or
farms in terms of pennylands. These subdivisions were often determined by geography but date back to Norse times and possibly earlier.
The structure of the rural economy had been stable for centuries, and
in 1748 we glimpse it just before collapse:

Alexander McEachan Tenant in Torbea (or Birchen hills) in
Arasaig Being Sworn and Examined Deposes That he possesses
without a Written Tack, a Seven Clitick or Seven Sixteenth parts
of a penny Land of said Town For Which he is lyable to pay
yearly Twenty One pounds fifteen Shilling Scotts of money Rent
& Converted Casualties and to free the Proprietor of the Kings
Cess and other publick Burdens Deposes that he possesses no
other Lands of the Estate of Clanronald and pays no more Rent
And that he ows no Rent preceeding Whitsunday last And this
he declares to be truth as he shall answer to God and Cannot
write.
     Donald McEachan Tenant in Torbea ... Deposes That it
Consists with his knowledge that Katharine McEachan and
Katharine Gillies Do each of them possess half a farthing Land
of Torbea For which each of them are lyable to pay yearly Six
pounds four shilling and Six pennies Scotts of money rent Including Converted Casualties and to free the Proprietor of the
Kings Cess and other publick Burdens Deposes that the said
Katharine McEachan and Katharine Gillies (who are both Infirm
and Cannot travell) do possess no other lands and pay no more
Rent And that to the best of his knowledge the said Katharine
McEachan is resting three years Rent at Whitsunday last, But,
that the s[ai]d Katharine Gillies rests no rent, haveing only

Entered at Whitsunday last, and this is truth as he shall answer
to God and Cannot write ...

John Kennedy and John McLeod Tenants in Ardgastrick in
Arasaig in the parish of Island Finan and Sheriffdome forsaid
Being Sworn and Examined Depose that they and Angus and
John McEachans also Tenants in Ardgastrick Do each of them
possess without a written Tack One farthing and one fourth part
of a farthing Land of said Toun For which each of them is lyable
to pay yearly Twelve pounds ten shilling Scotts of money Rent,
One pound five Shilling money forsaid for Butter & Cheese, and
One Weddor Sheep or two Merks Scotts for the same And to
free the Proprietor of the Kings Cess and other publick Burdens
Depose that they possess no other Lands of the Estate of Clan
Ranald, and pay no more rent than what is above mentioned
And that at Whitsunday last the said John McLeod was due two
years Rent of his possession, the said Angus McEachan one year
and the said John McEachan two years Rent But that the said
John Kennedy was due no Rent having only Entered at Whitsunday last And they declare the above to be truth as they shall
answer to God and that they Cannot write.

In the event the Clanranald estates were not forfeited but Bruce's
rental allows us to analyse the composition of the estate. Those parts
of the rental which had once been paid in kind had now been
converted into money. Since Culloden the arrears had accumulated,
no doubt because of the devastation caused by government forces.
The total Arisaig rental, including converted casualties, came to
c. £140 sterling whilst the arrears amounted to c. £66.

Arisaig was worth $32d$ – just more than the mediaeval valuation
which seems to have been at first 30 then 31 merklands. (The surviving
valuations suggest that the rate of exchange, according to the New
Extent, was 1 pennyland to 1 markland.) Two pennyworth were in
Clanranald's own hands. Seven families (nine tenants) were responsible for $11d$ or just over a third of what remained. Another 54 tenants
were responsible for $16.25d$ and there were $2.75d$ waste.

It is plain that rural society was highly structured. There were a
few men of substance, often tied to the chief's family by blood or
marriage, and there were lots of small tenants. Seventeen of them
occupied units of a farthing. Rents varied considerably; for some
reason they were much higher in the Brae of Arisaig (i.e. towards

Lochailort) than in Arisaig proper. There were four female tenants,
all of them old or infirm, and all with tiny parcels of land of 1/8d or
1/16d. There is little else we can say from such a list, except to
comment on how homogeneous such a society was. The five surnames of Macdonald, Maceachen, Gillies, Macinnes and Macgillivray
represent 81% of the total.

The Evidence from the 1762 North Morar Rental

We do not have so much detail for North Morar, but a surviving
rental from 1762 suggests a pattern of small tenancies with the land
running from generation to generation within one, two or three
families. Depending on the size of the settlement, the farmer might
have landless labourers working for him – to whom he could grant
some ground for potatoes and some grazing rights. The population
was distributed as in Map 6 where the prime determinant was
geography. Every bay on Loch Morar or Loch Nevis had its little
farm. There were 21 named settlements in the rental, and their
tenancies are best shown in tabular form.

Number of settlements		Number of tenants
6		1
11	(one of which is a father–son partnership)	2
1		3
3	(two of which list both father and son)	4

Figure 8 compares the various rentals we have for the district. The
rental for North Morar in 1762 is relatively high compared to Arisaig
in 1748. Arisaig was notionally worth two-and-a-half times as much.

Figure 8. Rental Increase in the Eighteenth Century

Estate	1699	1718	1748	1750	1762	1792	Source
Arisaig	c. £125						NAS, GD 201/1/362/3
Arisaig		c. £125					NAS, GD 201/5/1257/2
Arisaig			c. £140				NAS, E744/1/1
Arisaig & S.(?) Morar				c. £259			OSA
Arisaig & S. Morar						£1331	OSA
North Morar					c. £110		NLS, Delvine Papers, MS 1313

All rentals are in £ sterling. They are approximate since it is impossible to guarantee we are comparing like with like.
Arisaig does not here include Ardnish.

NAS = National Archives of Scotland (formerly the Scottish Record Office)
OSA = Old Statistical Account
NLS = National Library of Scotland

General Roy's Maps

Between Culloden and about 1755, General Roy conducted a military survey of the Highlands. The resultant map survives in two versions. The better known is the Fair Copy which is a coloured presentation map which, at some stage in its history, was cut into rectangular sections. This is very polished and visually attractive, but from the historian's point of view its lesser-known forerunner, the Protracted Copy, is more intriguing. This is the rough draft, full of extra pencil lines, errors and amendments. This too has been cut up – but into long thin strips. Plates 10 and 11 provide an example of each.

From the map we can actually tell where the surveyors worked. They must have travelled up the coast of Loch Nevis by boat, then inland from Mallaigvaig to Morar past Lochan Doilead (the Lily Pond). They went up Loch Morar by boat, and then down to Arisaig via Cross and Traigh. We can also tell what they did not survey. They did not go through to Loch an Nostarie by Glasnacardoch. This is a pity since there were undoubtedly settlements here and it would have helped us to date them. Traces of settlement appear on Boulton's map of 1834 but by this time the farms had already been abandoned.

Roy's map confirms the evidence from the rentals. The pattern of settlement was overwhelmingly coastal. Each farm consisted of two or three houses and a patch of arable land for crops. Few settlements were of any size since population numbers were closely tied to what the land could support.

In order to fill out this picture of the local economy I give some contemporary quotations. These are culled from the Statistical Accounts, David Bruce, Bishop Nicolson, Frogier de Kermadec etc. North Morar belonged to Glenelg parish, and South Morar and Arisaig to Ardnamurchan parish, which means they had separate entries in the Old and New Statistical Accounts.

Agriculture

North-morror is rocky and mountainous, mostly adapted for cattle ...

Seed Time and Harvest. – The oats are commonly sown in

the latter end of March and beginning of April; immediately thereafter the potatoes are planted, and then the barley ...

Grazing seems to be the only kind of farming for which this country is adapted; from necessity, and not choice, agriculture is carried on; the frequent rains, together with the inundations of the rivers, prove so destructive as to render the crops sometimes insipid and useless; but the price of meal ... will still urge them to continue their old method of farming with all its disadvantages, it being impossible to purchase the quantity required at such exorbitant prices. In the most favourable seasons, the crops raised are barely sufficient for the maintenance of their families during three-fourths of the year ...

Black Cattle and Sheep. – The cows in this parish are of a good kind, well shaped and piled, and being seldom housed, very hardy ...

The sheep are of the black-faced kind, and are thought to be good.

Rev Colin Maciver, *The Old Statistical Account for Glenelg*, 1793

The old rural economy of Arisaig and Morar is visible to anyone who walks. There are literally thousands of rigs and lazybeds littering the slopes of the area. These are both examples of ridge-and-furrow cultivation which is many centuries old and found throughout Europe. Rigs are the older and more universal form. Lazybeds (Gaelic *feannagan*) are a peculiarly Highland type where the thinness of the soil was overcome by adding a bed of seaweed and then heaping on top the soil which had been excavated from the ditch.

In terms of local practice I would distinguish rigs from lazybeds by their situation, shape and type of crop. The rigs on the farms tend to be wider (*c.* 3–4m), shallower and used for cereal crops such as oats or, occasionally, barley. They are typically found on more favourable ground and may be very ancient. Lazybeds are generally thinner (*c.* 2–3m), with a more pronounced ridge in the centre, and grew potatoes. Most can probably be dated to after 1750. They occur on some remarkably steep slopes and are often characterised today by a healthy growth of bracken.

In North Morar they are to be found above the raised beach at Glasnacardoch, on the slopes round Loch an Nostarie, east of Lochan Doilead, behind Bourblach and in dozens of other places as well. In most of these sites slope appears to have been more important than aspect. It was absolutely critical that the ground be well drained. The amount of sunlight seems to have been less important.

Most of these lazybeds were used as potato plots since few seem suitable for oats or barley. Potato planting in this part of the Highlands probably dates from about 1740, and in 1755 Mungo Campbell found that in Knoydart 'the raising of potatoes is much attended to by the whole inhabitants'. In 1773 Dr Johnson refers to potatoes as 'never wanting ... though they have not known them long'. The reason why Highlanders paid so much attention to cultivating potatoes is quite simple: they offered a much higher yield than grain crops where the return could be as low as three to one.

The vast number of lazybeds must be a symptom of a desperate hunger for land and a rapidly increasing population. We can probably date most of them to the period between 1750 and 1841, with the period of greatest use between 1770 and 1820. By 1841 there were only 24 people in Mallaig and four in Glasnacardoch, which doesn't suggest overcrowding. The cultivation of the numerous strips by Glasnacardoch and round Loch an Nostarie must have ended in an emigration about which we know nothing.

Graddan Meal

We glimpse the primitive rural economy of Arisaig and Morar in their method of grinding corn. Mills had been present in Scotland for hundred of years but for sound economic reasons were not common in the Highlands. It was not cost-effective to transport small quantities of grain to a distant mill. Boat journeys were risky, land journeys difficult. As a result most milling was done at home. To the improvers, this was anathema. Archibald Menzies describes the situation in Knoydart in 1768:

> They retain the barbarous custom of burning their straw in making graddan meal. The parts they don't burn they use as thatch to their houses. They usually pull their corns by the roots, cut of a part of the straw at top, which is burnt to dry their grain. The method of doing it is this. Two women sit down, each having a small stick in their hands. They set the straw on fire and, by turning it nimbly with their sticks and putting on more straw with corn, they take care not to burn the grain. Then they separate the grain from the ashes, put it into a tub, where

they rub it well with their hands & feet, and then winnow, clean & grind it in their querns, which are a kind of hand mills. From shearing their corns they will make bread in a few hours.

In 1772 Pennant refers to the same practice in Rum where:

Notwithstanding this island has several streams, here is not a single mill; all the molinary operations are done at home: the corn is 'graddaned', or burnt out of the ear, instead of being thrashed: this is performed two ways; first, by cutting off the ears, and drying them in a kiln, then setting fire to them on a floor, and picking out the grains, by this operation rendered as black as coal. The other method is more expeditious, for the whole sheaf is burnt, without the trouble of cutting off the ears: a most ruinous practice, as it destroys both thatch and manure, and on that account has been wisely prohibited in some of the islands ... They knead their bannock with water only, and bake or rather toast it, by laying it upright against a stone placed near the fire.

Both Menzies and Pennant regarded the custom as primitive and wasteful. In 1746 Frogier de Kermadec describes such a scene in Arisaig. He and some companions had gone ashore for an excursion whilst their cargo was unloaded. Curiosity drew them to a house from which escaped a lot of smoke. There they found six girls roasting oats:

who, seeing us, threw themselves into each other's arms and, whether they were ashamed of being seen poorly clad or whether they were afraid of us, wouldn't so much as look in our direction. I asked them in English what they wanted to make with these roasted oats, but, not making them do other than laugh like madmen, we were forced to leave them without being enlightened.

The Frenchmen learned later that the oats were burned to remove the grain. The women rubbed it with their feet in a sort of trough to separate the husk, then ground it, reduced it to the consistency of dough, and finally shaped it into flat cakes put to dry beside the fire. In the light of Archibald Menzies' description it is probable that Frogier disturbed some local girls making graddan meal. If they had been at the stage of rubbing it with their feet, it is likely they had their clothes hitched up, which would account for the giggling when their privacy was threatened by a party of French sailors.

Frogier's view of the resultant oatcakes was that they 'make the blackest and worst bread that one could ever eat'. The Highlanders, in contrast, reckoned 'this meal much better than any other'. A mill was built in Arisaig before 1763 but no doubt the remoter communities were slow to change.

Houses

Almost all West Highland houses in the eighteenth century were of the type known as creel houses. Bishop Nicolson's Report gives a good description of those in Strathglass:

> They are called Creil houses, because the larger timbers are interlaced with wickerwork in the same way that baskets are made. They are covered outside with sods, or divots. All the houses on the mainland, wherever we went, are built after this fashion, except those of the lairds and principal gentry.
>
> O Blundell, *Catholic Highlands of Scotland*, 1917

However, even some of the gentry lived in such houses. In 1803 James Hogg, the Ettrick Shepherd, described the house of Mr Mcdonald of Greenfield, Glengarry:

> The house was really a curiosity. It was built of earth, and the walls were all covered with a fine verdure, but on calling we were conducted into a cleanly and neat-looking room, having a chimney, and the walls being plastered. The ladies, Mrs Mc-Donald and her sister, were handsome and genteelly dressed ... They were very easy and agreeable in their manners, and very unlike the *outside* of their habitation.

Bishop Nicolson's Report also describes the shielings or temporary summer houses in Glengarry:

> Our ordinary lodgings on the journey were the shielings, or little cabins of earth four or five feet broad and six feet long, into which one enters by crouching on the ground, nor can one stand upright when arrived inside. These shielings the Highlanders use as shelters in the hills and forests, where they pasture their flocks, as also to store their dairy produce.
>
> O Blundell, *Catholic Highlands of Scotland*, 1917

The similarity of housing in the Rough Bounds is clear from Mungo Campbell's report on Knoydart in 1755–6:

> The whole houses of the country are made up of twigs manu-factured by way of creels called wattling and covered with turff. They are so low in the roof as scarce to admitt of a person standing in them, and when these are made up with pains they endure ten or twelve years. They thatch them [with] rushes.

The only modification that field-walking makes to this literary picture is that a number of local huts seem to have had stone footings, sometimes two or three courses high. Such a base would have been quick and easy to build and provided structural security for the wattle and turf walls. There are many such ruins amongst the abandoned farms of the area (see Plates 12 and 13).

They vary greatly in size, shape and method of construction. They are round, oval, rectangular, some with stone bases, some probably built entirely of turf and timber wattle, others entirely of stone. Many are beside arable ground, others at shieling sites, others completely isolated. As a rule the rectangular stone ruins are the most recent since such buildings only became common from the latter part of the eighteenth century. In 1793 the Old Statistical Account states that Arisaig and South Morar had only three slated houses built before 1780, with another eight built between then and 1793. The situation in North Morar would be similar.

Improvement

After about 1760 there is a good deal of evidence to show how the fever of agricultural improvement affected even the most remote Highland areas. We have details of a tack or lease from Clanranald to three tenants of Arieanskill in June 1761. This one-pennyland was set for ten years and their obligations included the following:

> to build their Dwelling houses of Stone within the Space of four years from their Entry to the Lands And to raise their march Dykes and other Dykes to inclose their farm of Stone where the same can be had convenient And of feall [turf] where Stone cannot be had and to plant such Inclosures with hedge or Trees either forrest or planting and to build their Kail Yards with a Stone Wall.

In contrast to the situation in 1748 when David Bruce often recorded that there was 'no written tack', we now have a cluster of tacks of which any improver would be proud. There is a tack in 1764 of Laggan, Ardnish, for five years, which is almost exactly the same as Arieanskill except for an added charge of 'Ten Shillings sterling for each tun of Kelp to be manufactured on the said farm'. The same day there is another tack of the two pennyland of Kinloid, written up by John Macdonald of Glenaladale, in almost precisely the same terms.

The tenants of Kinloid and Arieanskill were also under an obligation to take all their 'Grindable Corns' to the mill at Arisaig, so even the time-honoured custom of making graddan meal was under threat from within. In 1763 Ranald McDonald, 'Junior of Clanronald', set the mill of Ardnafuaran (claimed to be in good repair) in tack to one Donald Fraser, 'Together with the Change house of Ardnafuaran instantly and with all conveniency to be built by the said Ranald McDonald for the Entertainment of Strangers and Passengers'. And herein lies the origin of Arisaig Hotel!

Although the Clanranald estate had not been forfeited, there is little doubt that the clan authorities were emulating the 'improving' agenda that was being set on neighbouring estates. Barrisdale and Kinlochmoidart were now under government control, and the overall idea was for improvement of agriculture by encouraging individual responsibility, building dykes and stone houses, planting trees and hedges. The only respect in which the Clanranald leases were deficient is that they were not for sufficiently long periods of time.

In North Morar we find some evidence of improvement on the ground. In 1768 General Fraser bought the estate, perhaps partly as a source of recruits for the army, partly as a place to settle old soldiers who survived. There are five abandoned farms on the slopes around Loch an Nostarie. These have signs of rig-cultivation and most are enclosed by dykes. They are qualitatively distinct from the clusters of lazybeds found throughout the area and were probably intended to provide a full-time living. These are not patches of potato-ground with a few acres of grazing. That would never repay the effort of enclosure. They are symptomatic of the improver's outlook; a plot leased to an individual for a substantial term. They look like deliberate attempts to improve the rough muir. That they failed was more likely due to misplaced optimism than lack of effort.

They probably date to the period 1768–1800 when local recruits to the army, or their families, were enticed by the prospect of their own piece of ground. In return for a monumental expenditure of time and energy they would be granted a long lease to reap the rewards of their labour. However, it is likely that these lands were always marginal. They possibly survived until about 1815 although some may have succumbed more quickly. They may have been kept temporarily afloat by rising cattle prices during the Napoleonic Wars. They had been abandoned by 1841 – by which time there were only four families in Mallaig and one in Glasnacardoch.

Dykes

From the experiences of the factors of the Forfeited Estates in Knoy-dart it seems that march dykes were a rarity before the latter half of the eighteenth century. Boundaries were known by custom or oral tradition – which inevitably involved neighbours in disputes. The building of dykes was regarded as a hallmark of improvement and is helpful in dating changes in farm practice.

Dykes could be made of stone, turf (feal) or a mixture of turf and stone. It would be unwise to construct any great theory about the different materials in use since the important criterion was what was convenient. One late eighteenth-century farm in North Morar has a stone dyke on its rocky eastern perimeter, turf in its boggy north-western corner.

Walkers will occasionally come across the remains of a wire fence in the area. It might surprise them to know how old some of these are. In 1883 John Peter was discussing the enclosure of some crofts 'with a wire fence'. Apparently this had taken place two years earlier in 1881.

Trees

It is difficult to know just how much tree cover there once was in Arisaig and Morar. The destruction of woodland by a previous race is a not uncommon plea in the Highlands. In some areas the Vikings were anciently blamed for the removal of trees. The very existence of such forests, let alone their removal, may sometimes be a myth.

There has always been exploitation of woodland; the problem is whether natural regeneration matched this. There is also the issue of whether the heavy sheep stock that many Highland hills have carried for the last two centuries have worsened the matter. Not only do the animals graze closely but with them has developed a practice of indiscriminate muirburn to clear the ground for new grass. At the beginning of the nineteenth century Glengarry complained about the sheepfarmers burning the hills in springtime. He claimed that this muirburn killed the oak and birch that had been common in his youth.

We have only scraps of evidence to help us. Firstly we have place-names. Torr a' Bheithe, Druimindarroch, Eilean Giubhais etc. indicate the presence of birch, oak and Scots pine (*pinus sylvestris*) respectively. The problem is that we do not know when these names were first given and whether the woods they refer to were more extensive at the time. Moreover not all such names have survived onto today's maps. It is clear, though, that this was not an unbroken forest of Scots pine. Much of the local woodland was broadleaf and included birch, oak, hazel, alder and ash. In fact there are still healthy local stances of oak and birch.

In addition we have Bruce's Arisaig rental of 1748 which specifies the local woods and their value. We have some evidence from later tacks or leases which indicate a degree of landlord interest in local woodland. Then we have the maps, from Roy *c.* 1747–55, through Boulton in 1834, to the Ordnance Survey since 1873. These are important because they show remarkable consistency. The distribution of woodland as shown on Roy's map is strikingly similar to today's. Finally we have the anecdotal or topographical accounts. These are unscientific but give valuable impressions:

> John Gillies Ground Officer ... Deposes ... that there is the following Woods Vizt the Wood of Ardailish, The Wood of Larachmore, The Wood of Lochnanua, and the Wood of Strona-nushian, and Several Small Bushes of Wood in differrent parts of the Country ... Which haill Woods Consist of Oak, Ash, Birch, Hasel and Several other Sorts of Barren Timber.
>
> David Bruce, Arisaig Rental 1748

Bruce then appointed John MacDonald of Laig (Eigg), Aeneas MacDonald of Borrodale and Alexander MacDonald of Glen Beasdale to survey this woodland for him. They valued it at £1000 sterling which was a significant sum and approximately equal to seven years' rent of the whole Arisaig estate.

Conservation issues now found their way into tenancy agreements. In 1761 the tenants of Arieanskill were bound:

> to preserve the whole growing Timber on their farms from being destroy'd & from Cutting or peeling the same ... always allowing Wood Liberty for building of houses and other Labouring Utensils necessary for the use of the ground Firr, Oak Ash and Elm excepted.

As always, though, there were other pressures to exploit valuable resources. In 1772 a contract was drawn up between Ranald MacDonald of Clanranald and Messrs Hartlie and Atkinson of Netherhall Furnace, Cumberland, South Britain, for the supply of wood for making charcoal. Clanranald was to make over to them the woods of Moidart and Arisaig and in return Messrs Hartlie and Atkinson bound themselves

> to cutt down and manufacture at least Four hundred dozen Sacks of Charcoal out of the said woods annually and to continue to cutt down and manufacture the like Quantity of Four hundred dozen Sacks yearly till such time as the same are totally cutt down ... at the rate of Four shillings and Six pence Sterling for each of the said Four hundred dozen certain and every other dozen Sacks of Charcoal that shall be manufactured by them more than the above Quantity each Sack to be agreeable to practice Seven feet and a half long and three feet wide.

There was a clause retaining the more valuable timber:

> Excepting allways and Reserving all the Oaks, Elms and Ash in the said woods and also Reserving such parts or parcells thereof as may be deemed necessary for the use of the Tenants or Farmers on the Estates

Nevertheless one is left with the feeling that conservation was less important to Clanranald than profit.

Hugh Cheape has also drawn attention to the management of the woodland resources on the Clanranald Estates. These came under increasing pressure in the eighteenth century. On the one hand there are responsible tenancy agreements and indications that the authorities were aware of the need for conservation. On the other there are contracts such as that to Netherhall Furnace in 1772 or the Lorn Furnace in 1794.

It is not possible to arrive at a balanced conclusion because we do not know the former state of the woodland, what degree of exploitation was sustainable and how much was actually cut down. However, we are left with a suspicion that whilst conservation issues were well-aired, short-term pressures were probably decisive. In this respect the woodlands on the Forfeited Estates may have fared better than those which remained under private ownership. The former sometimes benefited from a degree of benign paternalism, the latter, as Clanranald's, were expendable in order to maintain the dignity of the chiefly family.

The above reports apply more particularly to Arisaig. With regard to Morar we have the comments of John Leyden, an early traveller, who was viewing North Morar from Loch Nevis:

> Morar is only distinguished by the superior height of its mountains. It is naked of trees, and consists of a vast sheet of heath spread over a great extent of rocky mountains and eminences ...
>
> We learned that the ancient wicker houses of the Highlanders promoted in no inconsiderable degree the destruction of these forests ...
>
> The view of the lake here is exceedingly wild and romantic. The hills by which it is confined consist entirely of gray rocks and heath, skirted here and there with strips of thin wood where formerly flourished extensive and almost impenetrable forests.
>
> John Leyden, 1800

We should perhaps be sceptical of Leyden's claim of a former forest. The wattle used for creel huts certainly required pliant young saplings, but since the huts were small and lasted 10–12 years each, it is feasible that natural regeneration matched any consumption for house-building. The comments of the Knoydart factors show that the free roaming of cattle and goats also damaged young trees – as did visiting fishermen. The evidence from the Old Statistical Account for Glenelg suggests that peat was normally used for fuel. It was relatively convenient and wood was probably recognised as too valuable. Whilst admitting damage from house-building, grazing animals and fishermen, it is unlikely that North Morar's small population placed an undue burden on the native tree cover.

Boulton's map of 1834 provides further evidence of a general absence of trees in North Morar. For much of the western knuckle his comments are of the type 'Rough, rocky Ground covered with heath' or 'A steep naked rocky face'. His views are supported by the Description of North Morar in the 1841 Census return:

> This district is bounded on 3 sides by the sea and consists entirely of rocky hills, some of these are mere naked rocks while others are partially clothed with a meagre and stunted vegetation.

It is either the case that much of North Morar was never covered in trees; or these were lost long before 1834. It would be difficult to blame sheep for this since North Morar had not yet been transformed into a sheep-run. (The 1841 enumerator specifically commented on the limited amount of sheep farming in the district.) Assuming that North Morar's population was always modest − because of the poverty of the land − it would be difficult to claim that Man was responsible for much destruction. North Morar in past centuries may have looked much as it does now.

Fishing

Eighteenth-century commentators had a keen eye for economic opportunities. Industries which offered potential were kelp, fishing and cattle-droving. Kelp and droving did spectacularly well when prices rose during the Napoleonic wars. For a short period Clanranald made a fortune out of kelp. Unfortunately, much of this new-found wealth was then spent elsewhere. After Waterloo the prices of both commodities collapsed and the Highland economy was again in crisis.

One of the perennial chestnuts of Highland history is to know why the fishing industry did not establish itself locally before the nineteenth century. There had always been fishing here, but in early times it was usually exploited by people from outwith the Highlands. John Knox offered his views on the subject in 1786. He regarded fish as the most important economic resource in the area:

> the great varieties of fish which are found in the lakes, channels, and seas of the Highlands, may be considered as the grand natural staple of that country, exceeding in value all the other resources united

Firstly he detailed the overall problems of the area:

Thus we find that the Highlands, besides supplying home demands, exports fish, black cattle, horses, sheep, timber, bark, lead, slate, and kelp; to which may be added sundry articles of less importance, as skins, feathers, oil.

The aggregate amount of these exports is surely sufficient to procure the necessary articles of grain, and various utensils in iron, steel, timber, etc. wherewith to improve their lands, extend their fisheries, furnish themselves with decked vessels, and erect more comfortable dwellings.

Such are the specific wealth and the specific wants of the Highlands. But as the value of its natural produce, by sea and land, is almost wholly absorbed by the great landholders, and by many of them spent at Edinburgh, London, Bath, and elsewhere; as the people are thus left more or less at the mercy of stewards and tacksmen, the natural resources of the country, instead of a benefit, become a serious misfortune to many improveable districts. Those who, by their education and their knowledge of the world might diffuse general industry, and raise a colony of subjects, useful to their king, to their country, and to themselves, are the very persons who glean these wilds of the last shilling, and who render the people utterly unqualified for making any effectual exertions in any case whatever.

Knox lists a number of specific problems faced by the fishing industry in the Highlands. There were difficulties in the supply of salt for preserving the fish and there was bureaucratic interference from Customs House officials. There were great disturbances between the busses from the Clyde and the Highlanders (the former had the resources, the latter had the local knowledge). Locals lacked decked vessels and as a result only caught sufficient for their own needs. Landowners stifled every attempt by their tenants to improve themselves; there were legal restrictions in connection with the bounty system; piers were absent and freight costs high.

He pointed out the vicious circle of poverty in which the Highlanders were caught. They could not afford the capital outlay that was necessary to help them break out of the poverty trap. But there was another issue which was a powerful hindrance to progress. Highland society was strictly hierarchical. There were no towns or industries, and few merchants or artisans. If the landowner did not foster improvement or progress, then no one else was in a position to do

so. Highland society was unsuited to support such a capitalist and
individualist industry as fishing.

Knox's fourth most favoured site for a fishing village on mainland
Scotland was *Lochnanuach* (Loch nan Uamh). Unfortunately he does
not discuss this area specifically in the text, but he comments on the
fact that many types of fish had no market:

> Haddocks and whitings are found in such abundance in the lochs,
> as well as the main sea, that scarcely any value is set upon them
> in the Highlands ... Mackarel come periodically, in mighty
> shoals; but these are also despised, though capable of being cured
> for exportation ... Shell fish, as lobsters, oysters, crabs, clams,
> mussels, cockles, bring no price, and consequently incite no
> attention, though it is well known that some of these fish might
> be pickled and exported.

This was strongly endorsed by later commentators:

> Skate, ling, and cod are to be got along the coast of the parish,
> but sythe or pollock is caught in the greatest abundance, which
> in summer is chiefly the support of the poor people ...
>
> It is computed for some years back 30,000 barrels [of herring]
> have been annually caught in this loch [Hourn]; but the want of
> salt prevents the natives from turning to advantage this bounty
> of Providence, which from their local situation they might other-
> wise do; at present, they are content with fishing a barrel or two
> to help the maintenance of their families.
>
> Rev Colin Maciver, Old Statistical Account for Glenelg, 1793

> The sea along the coast, and the various lochs branching off
> from it, have long been famed for the number and quality of
> herrings frequenting them; but, of late years, the fishing has
> failed, as on all the west coast of Scotland, to the impoverishment
> of a large population who subsisted by it. Other fish are caught
> to the extent used by those employed in taking them, and the
> supply required by the country, – the prevalent kinds being ling
> and cod; but few, if any, are exported.
>
> Rev Alexander Beith, New Statistical Account for Glenelg,
> 1836

> The fisheries of cod and ling, and other fishes caught by the
> hook, on the north coasts of the parish, promise, at some future

period, to prove a plentiful source of industry. They are, however, at present merely in their infancy as branches of traffic, though considerable quantities of such fishes are obtained by the inhabitants as food for their families.

Rev Angus M'Lean, New Statistical Account for Arisaig, 1838

The British Society for Extending the Fisheries, for whom Knox wrote, eventually set up a station at Ullapool. The Commissioners for the Forfeited Estates tried to encourage an industry in Knoydart, sadly without long-term success. In the 1840s Lord Lovat laid the foundation for what was to become the economic cornerstone for North Morar – a fishing village in Mallaig. The opportunities were seen in the eighteenth century but, for a variety of reasons, the fishing industry got off to a slow start in the Highlands. The business of distribution was not really solved until the twentieth century and the coming of the railway.

Emigration

Emigration and clearance are twin symptoms of the Highland problem after Culloden. They have a vast literature of their own, so in this chapter I confine myself to their occurrence in Arisaig and Morar. Arisaig offers a good example of emigration being organised by the Highlanders themselves. In this case it was driven by senior cadets of Clanranald who were unhappy with the clan leadership and tried to preserve the integrity of Highland society in a new context – North America. The best summary of local reasons for emigration is given by Rev Colin Maciver, Glenelg, writing for the Old Statistical Account in 1793:

Emigration is thought to be owing in a great measure to the introduction of sheep, as one man often rents a farm where formerly many families lived comfortably; ... But this is not solely the cause; the high rents demanded by landlords, the increase of population, and the flattering accounts received from their friends in America, do also contribute to the evil.

Many causes have been offered for this surge in population – the ending of clan warfare, the introduction of potatoes, inoculation against smallpox etc. Individually none of these is completely convincing but the fact is that Highland population rose steeply in the period 1750–1831. It is possible the process may have started before this but we are hampered by the lack of reliable demographic data before about 1755. Unfortunately population increase was not matched by a parallel increase in resources. The Highland economy could cope if cattle and kelp fetched high prices, if potato crops were good, if the herring came, if the men found employment in the army. Not all of these conditions obtained all of the time. During the Napoleonic wars prices rose steeply, but during peacetime, or when the potatoes or herring failed, the problems became acute.

Highland rural society was completely hierarchical, and different chiefs responded in different ways to the endemic problems of over-population and an impoverished agricultural base. In general terms rents shot up, sheep were introduced, and tenants came under increasing economic pressure – although the details varied from area to area (see Figures 7 and 8). There was a changed relationship between chief and clansman, the loss of any community of interest. Tenants came to be seen as liabilities rather than assets. Ever since, the landlords have been heavily criticised for abandoning any patriarchal interest in their people and adopting an 'economic' approach. In the context of Arisaig we can regard it as fair criticism because it was voiced by senior members of the clan themselves.

In 1771–2 John Macdonald of Glenaladale and his brother Donald organised a major emigration from the Clanranald estates. Iain Mackay has given some details of this process by publishing a letter from John Macdonald dated March 1772. It was written to his relative Alexander (Alasdair an Oir), a son of Angus Macdonald of Borrodale. John had suffered some differences with the family of Clanranald which:

> made me wish for a feasible Method of leaving the inhospitable Part of the World, which has fallen to our share ... Yet all the Countrys round thought me extravagant & mad, & indeed blamed me exceedingly for thinking to invite any person to Such a wretchid place in every respect as they described the Island of St John to be ... Several Settlers have agreed to goe to our Lot – Our Method is to give them by Lease for ever a certain Number of Acres, such as they can manage easily, they paying us a small yearly Quitrent out of it, & furnishing themselves all necessarys & Passage, only that we must direct & Assist them to carry it on – A Number of other people & our own friends have joined

After this Manner to the Number of 214 Souls, Men, Women & Children ... It is a most expencive Project, requiring a vast Sight of ready Money, but I hope to get it gone thro, tho with difficulty – Emigrations are like to demolish the Highland Lairds, & very deservedly.

Even Angus Macdonald of Borrodale, Bonnie Prince Charlie's 'faithfull old Landlord', had lost something of his Jacobite fervour:

He is positive this Scheme was inspired by Providence – It would make you laugh to hear how he Applys to this case, the Story of Jacob, Joseph, Egypt, Moses, etc., etc.; in different ways – It has driven the Pretender out of his Nodle entirely : He never speaks of him now, & he is quit a good Subject.

Glenaladale remained in Scotland for the moment,

receiving Such Opprest people as offer themselves to us from all Corners, but certain it is I cannot be fond of the Country after all those I love best are away – Having a greater Interest now in St John than in the Lands I have at home – It being a much better Climate & Country ... We have a very Severe winter, last harvest failed entirely : Meal is scarce and ... Cattle will be lost, & of Small Price under these Circumstances they have No reason to regret it who leave the Highlands.

Fortunately some of the documents relating to these arrangements still survive in Canada. Figure 9 gives details of an indenture made between the Glenaladale brothers and Donald Gilles of Brinacory in North Morar. Beneath the legal language we can sense the opportunity available for Donald. In return for six years of his life he could look forward to two hundred acres of North America. We know from Boulton's map of 1834 that Brinacory offered only meagre pockets of arable land. In Morar, life could never be less than harsh. Who could ever blame Donald, or all the others since?

The tale of emigration continues. In 1790 three ships, the *Jane*, the *Lucy* and the *British Queen*, sailed from Arisaig to Canada. Their human cargo included 176 from Arisaig and North Morar, more than one-tenth of the total population. In 1801 another 59 went on the *Dove* and the *Sarah*. We are fortunate to have surviving passenger lists for these vessels which specify where the individual families came from. In 1802 the *Neptune* sailed from Loch Nevis with 600 passengers, doubtless including many from Morar.

Figure 9. Indenture and Tack Twixt Donald Gilles in Brunacory in Moror And John & Donald Macdonalds 1771

It is contracted, Indented and finally agreed betwixt John Macdonald Esquire of Glenalladale and Donald Macdonald his Brother German on the one part and Donald Gilles in Brunacory in north Moror on the other part That is to say The said Donald Gilles hereby becomes bound servant to the said John and Donald Macdonalds their heirs Administrators and Assigns for the full and complete space of six years after his entry which is hereby declared to begin and commence from and after the twelfth of May last ... [1771] and the said Donald Gilles Binds and Obliges him during that space faithfully and truly to attend and serve his said masters at any work they shall find necessary to employ him in at all times by night and by day, work day, holyday and not to absent himself during that space therefrom without his masters or their overseers leave first asked and given and that he shall chearfully and willingly obey his said masters or overseers lawfull orders and commands and also that he shall not willingly hear or see any hurt or prejudice to his said masters in their name or Effects, but shall hinder and impede the same to the utmost of his power and timeously acquaint them therewith and further that he shall not reveal nor divulge any secrets wherewith he shall be entrusted by his said masters and moreover that he shall not embezzle or fraudulently put away any of his said masters goods or Effects and others belonging to them and on the other part The said John and Donald Macdonalds Bind and Oblige them their heirs and Executors to pay the charges of Bringing the said Donald Gilles to the Island of St John in North America and Likeways to pay him Three pounds Sterling besides his maintainance yearly for the first two years and Four pounds Sterling yearly during the remainder of the said term of six years also Also at the end of said term to give him possession Two hundred acres of Land which they hereby Demise sett and to farm Lett to him, his heirs and assigns from and after the term of Whitsunday next after the Expiry of this Indenture for the space of two thousand nine hundred and ninety six years Saving and Reserving to his Majesty his heirs and Successors all rights and priviledges Saved and Reserved in the Originall grants of the Lott wherein the said two hundred acres shall happen to be given wherefore The said Donald Gilles Binds and Obliges him his heirs Executors and Administrators to pay unto the said John and Donald MacDonald their heirs Executors, Administrators and Assigns on the fifteenth day of May one thousand seven hundred and seventy eight one penny sterling for each of said acres for the preceeding year the like sum for each Acre for the year thereafter, after which to pay three pence Sterling per acre yearly for seven years, thereafter to pay six pence Sterling per Acre yearly for seven years more at the end of which to pay one shilling sterling per acre yearly for ten years and afterwards to pay one shilling and six pence sterling per acre during the remainder of said two thousand nine hundred and ninety six years and that over and above the Quittrents and Taxes imposed or to be imposed on the said Lands and Lastly both parties bind and oblige them to implement fullfill and perform their respective parts of the premises to each other under the penalty of Thirty pounds Sterling to be paid by the party failing to the party observing or willing to observe their part of the premises. In witness whereof both parties have hereunto sett their hands and Seals and unto another Duplicate hereof this.

Public Archives and Records Office of Prince Edward Island, Accession No. 2664, Item No. 138

It is all very well bewailing this emigration, but many of these families were economic migrants who chose to leave Britain for better opportunities elsewhere. The motives of the landowners seldom bear scrutiny, but as for the migrants themselves – who can blame them? This process is universal. It is part and parcel of the relationship between different economies over space and time. New economic orders expose structural weaknesses in traditional societies. The process of adjustment is inevitable and continuous. Sometimes, as in the Highlands, it is costly in terms of social dislocation and tragic in terms of culture loss.

CHAPTER 7

THE MILITARY TRADITION

There was a long and deep-rooted military tradition in the Highlands. For several hundred years men from the Highlands and Islands engaged as mercenaries in Ireland, quite apart from their numerous armed encounters with each other and Lowland Scots. Such service is a recurrent theme throughout the Middle Ages and was only ended by the Union of Crowns in 1603. Whether or not the primary reason for this was economic necessity the fact remains that militarism became a significant aspect of Highland culture. A report, written after Bishop Nicolson's visitation to the area in 1700, draws attention to this:

> They are much given to following the military profession; their character, the roughness of their land, and their manner of life render them well suited to it. There is not the humblest peasant but has his sword, his musket, his targe and a large dirk, which is always to be seen hanging at his side. Besides these arms the gentry use helmets and breastplates.
>
> O Blundell, *Catholic Highlands of Scotland*, 1917

This evidence is confirmed by the diary of William Frogier de Kermadec, ensign on the French privateer the *Mars*. The *Mars* and the *Bellone* were two French ships which arrived in Loch nan Uamh shortly after the battle of Culloden. They carried a cargo of money and arms which they hastily disembarked. During this process Frogier had a brief respite and so he and some companions went ashore. Extracts from his diary have been printed by L. A. Boiteux and are valuable since they refer specifically to the residents of Arisaig. Frogier was struck both by the poverty and the warlike aspect of the High-landers. Armed with musket, pistols, sword and dirk, they knew no other profession than war: 'They have a very thieving spirit and no other religion than that which Nature teaches them'.

We also have a list, made up in 1745, of men who enrolled from Clanranald's Moidart estate. The names of 80 men appear, 79 of whom have an entry made against them. Of these, 15 had no weapons at all. The remaining 64 had 49 guns, 48 swords, seven shields and a pistol among them. Alexander Macdonald, the poet, is listed under Dalilea and is the only man in the roll to possess a pistol, as well as a gun. In the Rough Bounds a high proportion of disposable income was invested in weaponry.

This mix of military prowess, economic hardship and a sense of cultural identity meant that the 'Highland problem' troubled Lowland Scotland from the Treaty of Perth to the Battle of Culloden. Some Scottish kings, like James IV, tackled the Highlanders head on, but this was an expensive and risky course of action. Many favoured the classic policy of divide-and-rule, utilising some clans, such as the Campbells, against others. Whilst the Highlands could be overawed, they were never comprehensively reduced. By itself the Lowland Scottish state lacked the resources for a long war of attrition.

Unrest flourished during the civil conflicts of the seventeenth century, and it wasn't until 1746 that the Highlanders met with overwhelming defeat at Culloden. The political and military repression that followed left the Highlands unable to oppose the British state, and what is extraordinary is that within two generations they were fighting so fiercely for it. Many of the Highland emigrants of the 1770s fought for Britain as Loyalists during the American War of Independence.

Highland regiments were raised for Britain's foreign wars from the latter half of the eighteenth century onwards. In political and military terms this represented an extraordinary triumph for the British body politic. Pitt's boast about absorbing the military spirit of the clans into the British army rings true. The motives of some politicians may not have been of the noblest since they undoubtedly viewed Highland regiments as cheap and expendable. Nevertheless the problem of Highland military opposition was finally overcome, with the bonus that the Highlanders made brave soldiers. The relationship between the Highlands and the rest of Scotland, and then Britain, had been a political problem from 1266 until 1746. This issue was resolved at Culloden. The military challenge was defeated, then absorbed. However, the economic causes of the Highland problem have never been tackled.

Of course it was not an easy road for Highlanders. Many were killed or died of disease in foreign lands. There were difficulties over the raising of Catholic regiments and the advancement of Catholic officers. Highland regiments were callously disbanded when peace broke out, ruthlessly exploited in times of need. However, Highland soldiers had been fighting as mercenaries in Ireland for hundreds of years. Now they were serving under their chiefs who were officers in the British Army. It was not perhaps a very attractive policy, but in political terms it was wonderfully expedient. From being a mortal enemy of the British state in 1746, Highland regiments became one of its bastions against Napoleon at the end of the century. How did it affect our area?

In 1768 General Simon Fraser purchased the estate of North Morar from Macdonell of Glengarry. No doubt part of his rationale was for new tenants to support his military and political ambitions. He would be able to recruit locally and reward his men with pockets of land as and if they survived to become old soldiers. Recruitment was not a matter of volunteering. This was the era of the press-gang, and the realities of land-tenure in the Highlands meant recruiting by coercion. In 1794, when Macdonell of Glengarry found his tenants in Knoydart reluctant to enlist in his new regiment, he wrote furiously to his Inverness agent and demanded their immediate eviction. Soldiers were 'volunteered' by families as a matter of financial necessity. The economic and cultural background would not permit freedom of choice as we imagine it today. An anonymous report of 1750, probably by David Bruce, describes 'what the Highlanders call a following, that is a Clannish Right to oblige the Common People to rise in Arms, whenever they please to call them'.

We learn of a nameless recruit from Stoul in 1786 and, from the Canadian records, of a Captain Donald Gillis of Stoul. According to the Old Statistical Account for Ardnamurchan (1795), there were 50 soldiers from Arisaig and South Morar 'in the army this war'. There was also George Macdonell, son of John Macdonell of Finiskaig, who became a Lieutenant in the Bengal Native Infantry and died in Calcutta in 1818.

In his book *Moidart*, Rev Charles Macdonald paints an attractive portrait of another local soldier, Colonel Gillis of Kinlochmorar. Despite being born to a very poor family he rose through the ranks and retired to Kinlochmorar where he built a house. He was apparently rather eccentric and something of a storyteller. He is buried in the tiny graveyard at Meoble pier. That the practice of soldiering continued well into the nineteenth century is evident from the census returns. In 1851 three paupers are described as 'soldier's wives'.

Quite apart from the fortunes or otherwise of individual recruits there is the broader impact of this process on the gradual political and social inclusion of Highlanders and Highland culture within the British state. Two hundred and fifty years after being proscribed as instruments of war, there is probably no safer home for the bagpipe and kilt than within the regiments of the British Army. How did this extraordinary turnaround occur? Evidence from an Arisaig family can illuminate a process which was well under way within two generations of Culloden.

The following quotations come from letters written by Captain John Macdonald to his father, Archibald Macdonald of Rhu, during the Peninsular Wars. Archibald's father, John Macdonald, had been one of Bonnie Prince Charlie's most faithful adherents. John was son of Angus Macdonald of Borrodale whom Charles used to call his 'faithfull old Landlord'. John himself had helped guide the Prince through the government cordon that threatened to trap him in the west. So here was young John, fighting courageously for the very army against which his grandfather had campaigned in 1745 (see Figure 10).

Captain John had joined up in 1810 and was commissioned into the 23rd Foot (Royal Welch Fusiliers). After service in Guernsey he was sent to Iberia where he served in Wellington's army. His letters

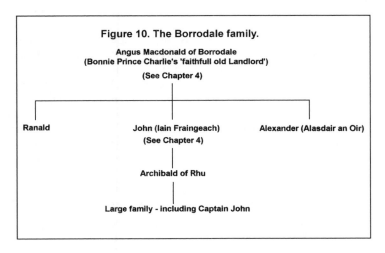

Figure 10. The Borrodale family.

Angus Macdonald of Borrodale
(Bonnie Prince Charlie's 'faithfull old Landlord')

(See Chapter 4)

Ranald

John (Iain Fraingeach)
(See Chapter 4)

Alexander (Alasdair an Oir)

Archibald of Rhu

Large family - including Captain John

home were retained by his family and edited by Father Macdonald, author of *Moidart*, who had hoped to publish them as a sequel to his own book. Charles Macdonald died before this could be achieved but his edition was eventually published in the *Celtic Monthly* (1904).

These letters give a fascinating account of a young man's experience of war and his observations on those around him. But equally his correspondence reveals the subtle ambiguities of his position. He would, no doubt, incur the wrath of many Scots today by his unconscious adoption of the term 'English' to describe his army and himself. But, at the same time he retained his clannishness. His letters are full of references to the other Highlanders in the Army. He was concerned for their welfare and proud of their achievements. He not only embodies the unconscious arrogance of the British, who regard all other peoples as somehow less favoured, but also makes frequent reference to the admirable performance of his 'countrymen', by which he means Highlanders.

This blithe disregard for the contradictions of his own position, his ability to accommodate them, are a sign of the achievement of the British state in its period of expansion. Somehow the concept of Britain engaged the energies and loyalty of this young Highlander. John participated in a British institution, and this British overlay on his cultural identity is important although unstated. Admittedly, war induced a sense of cohesion in the face of common danger. Nevertheless, the contradictions which Captain John managed to overcome, have resonated ever since and are today not always so happily resolved.

His letters are full of news of his fellow Highlanders. Writing of Colonel Donald McDonell, Santaig, whom he met in Portugal, he says: 'He is as fat and fair as if he had just arrived from England'. Of others such as young Allan from Inverailort: 'Allan Kinachreggan has grown remarkably tall, and is a fine young man. The Eigg lads are both well. Cameron, Strone, I see every day as he is in the same brigade. Macdonald, Knock, is quite well'. Of a Lieutenant MacDougall who had recently arrived: 'We have got a fine young grenadier from Lorn out here the other day; I have got him to my company'.

But of course John was taking part in a bitter war against the French. In November 1812 he describes a long retreat:

For the last month we have been constantly moving without any covering, and often without any baggage, in the worst weather possible, and the roads as deep as any part of the moss at Bunacaime [The boggy ground around the mouth of the River Cam between Traigh and Back of Keppoch]. It is the first time I have been in a serious retreat and I hope it shall be the last. The scenes of misery met with every day exceeded anything I would have imagined. Men, women, and children, together with every sort of beast of burden, dropping down on all sides – starving with hunger and cold, and no one able to give the least possible relief.

By February 1813 he was in a happier frame of mind:

We now no longer feel any bad effects from our late retreat. I enjoy the best of health. We are in the centre of the country where you get all your port wine from, and which is infinitely better here – not having been mixed with any spiritous liquors. The country is perhaps wilder than any part of the Highlands, and though the tops of the mountains are constantly covered with snow, we enjoy during the daytime the mildness of summer ... I am learning the Spanish language from a friar who was turned out of Salamanca by the French, and who speaks English remarkably well.

By July 1813 he was involved in the thick of the action against the French in the Pyrenees:

How any of us got out of this action is to me astonishing, as we were for six or seven hours exposed to the most tremendous fire possible. My captain was killed, and the other lieutenant wounded, so that I have got the grenadier company ever since ... I write this on the top of a bleak hill, without any covering, and on my knees.

John himself had a narrow escape at Salamanca. He was knocked down by a spent bullet which hit him in the stomach: 'The bullet hit on the knot of my sash which was luckily tied in front, and did not penetrate the skin!' But not everybody was so fortunate. Writing of the death of the young son of Colonel Macdonald, Inch, of the 92nd he says: 'Poor Inch was much affected at his son's death. He recovered the body next day after a long search, and buried it in a decent manner.'

And in January 1814 John writes of the death of Allan Macdonald, Kinachreggan:

> He received a musket-ball through the heart, while gallantly leading on his company to the charge, and never spoke afterwards. He was buried next morning on the ground where he fell ... His poor father must suffer much from such an accumulation of misfortunes. Perhaps the knowledge of his son's uniform good and gallant conduct may tend to alleviate the grief at his loss.

On the Spanish troops fighting for the French: 'We have not fallen in with any of them as yet, but our men laugh at the idea of calling them soldiers, seeing the manner in which those on our side fight'. Whilst of those on the British side:

> The great numbers we have lost in the retreat from fatigue and hunger, ... have weakened the army so considerably that it is rendered unfit for any active service for some time. To remedy the great loss of men last year, we are to have a Spanish brigade attached to each division, and give them English officers, which is the only chance of doing any good. At present they are quite a burlesque on soldiers. The Portuguese are much better, having been disciplined by English officers, but even they cannot be made to charge.

It is interesting to hear John's rationalisation of the poor performance of the Spanish troops: '... the Spaniards ... did not behave very well; but we must forgive them as they are but young soldiers'.

John, like other Highlanders, felt that military qualities were bred by usage. In his report on the Highlands in 1750, David Bruce comments that because the ordinary people of Moray have 'been for a long time disused from Arms they are not reckoned a good Militia'. He goes on to say something similar about the inhabitants of Banff, Aberdeen, Kincardine, and Angus. Bruce also claimed that about 1730 Cameron of Lochiel had tried to convert his people from cattle-thieving. Apparently the neighbouring chiefs dissuaded him on the grounds that it was necessary for the Jacobite cause that his men 'be kept in the use of Arms'. The tradition had to be maintained if it was to be called upon.

John's pride was always stirred by the exploits of his fellow-Highlanders: 'You would have observed ... how severely our countrymen suffered throughout the whole of the operations. Their conduct is the universal theme of admiration in the whole army'.

Critics of Highland soldiers only ever despaired of their discipline – or lack of it. It is curious therefore to hear what this Highland officer had to say of the virtues of military discipline during a battle in front of Toulouse on 10 March 1814:

> I am sorry the loss fell particularly on our countrymen who, on this occasion, even surpassed their former good conduct ... Our brigade did not suffer very much ... but we had two or three opportunities of showing our coolness, in forming squares against cavalry, etc.

At the Battle of Vittoria the French were defeated and John writes ruefully of his inability to take the opportunity of growing rich by plunder, not least because of the close attendance of Wellington, who wished to capitalise on the pursuit of the enemy. It is ironic to compare John's description of the victor's spoils with one given by an officer in Cumberland's army after Culloden. Large quantities of livestock, some of it undoubtedly from Arisaig and Morar, were sold off at Fort Augustus:

> Whilst our Army stayed here, we had near twenty Thousand Head of Cattle brought in, such as Oxen, Horses, Sheep, and Goats, taken from the Rebels ... so that great Numbers of our Men grew rich by their Shares in the Spoil, ... the Money was divided amongst the Men, and few Common Soldiers were without Horses.
>
> 　　　　　*A Journey through part of England and Scotland by a*
> 　　　　　　　　　　　　　　　　　　　*Volunteer,* 1747

Unfortunately for John, he could not make Vittoria compensate for Culloden:

> The quantity of baggage taken is enormous, and though our division was the first that passed over it, yet from having his Lordship along with us, and from the quickness of the pursuit we had no time to plunder. We repeatedly saw carts and waggons loaded with plate and silver, without a man falling out of the ranks to lay hands on it. Again, there was money, jewels, luxuries of every description strewn about the roads and lanes without a possibility of our falling out of the ranks to pick them up. The

division in our rear got an immense quantity, some officers having secured from eight to ten thousand dollars ... Our camp next morning more resembled a Fair than a regular encampment, every man selling or buying some article of plunder. My own share is a mule.

This remark of John's brings us full circle. For centuries Highlanders had been driven, by economic necessity, to raiding and warfare. Throughout the Middle Ages, fleets of Highland and Hebridean galleys carried mercenaries to Ireland. There they fought for the Irish against other Irish or the English. That ended with the Union of Crowns in 1603. At home they raided each other or the Lowlands. That ended with Culloden. From now on their energies were harnessed to a new order. The power of the chief as military leader was over. Nevertheless a number of the chiefs went on to exercise military leadership within the British Army, a tradition that was still going in the twentieth century.

CHAPTER 8

THE NINETEENTH CENTURY

If the eighteenth century saw the political despatch of the old Highland order, then the two centuries since have seen its economic transformation. Culturally it was still largely intact in 1891 but enormous economic changes had already taken place. These changes occurred in different ways in different districts. This chapter is only concerned with the principal factors at work in Arisaig and Morar. Some of these were unique, but many were shared with the wider Highland world.

Sources

Far more evidence is available for this period than for any previous century. Moreover this evidence is not just accidental or anecdotal; official records began to be maintained. From 1800 the government ran a decennial census although until 1841 the returns were only in the form of a summary count. From 1841 to 1891 they contain full details of individuals, along with place of residence, occupation etc. These are a mine of information and allow comparison with earlier documents such as the Old Statistical Account. Records of Births, Deaths and Marriages were officially kept from 1855 but we also have the Morar Parish Baptismal and Marriage Records which begin in 1832 and 1833 respectively.

From 1836 we have the New Statistical Account for Glenelg, written by Rev Alexander Beith, followed by that for Ardnamurchan drawn up by Rev Angus M'Lean in 1838. In 1846–7 there was the potato famine and a good deal of interest in the Highland predicament. In 1848 Robert Somers visited the area and included a chapter on Arisaig in his *Letters from the Highlands*. Towards the end of the century there were two Royal Commissions which enquired into conditions in the Highlands. On 6 August 1883 the Napier Commission sat in

Arisaig, asked about 600 questions and took evidence running to
nearly 39 pages. In August 1894 the Deer Forest Commission came
to Arisaig, asked some 850 questions and produced another 22 pages
of closely-written evidence.

I have made no attempt to reproduce this body of raw data. There
is far too much of it and the wealth of detail can quickly become
confusing. However, in the Bibliography I have given some sources
for those who wish to pursue matters further. The two Royal
Commissions were events of great drama. Beneath the calm and
orderly proceedings, beneath the Victorian thoroughness and attention
to detail, we can sense the momentous occasion. After years of struggle
for land reform the government was listening. But it was not easy.
The questioning was close, searching, and sometimes hostile. There
was an atmosphere of the courtroom where little passed unchallenged.
On the Napier Commission sat sympathetic Highlanders like Fraser-
Mackintosh, but also landowners like Cameron of Lochiel. In the
case of the Deer Forest Commission, Mr Nicholson, husband of the
owner of Arisaig, was permitted to cross-question the witnesses but
the courtesy was not reciprocated. The system was still heavily loaded.

In order to process this mass of information I have addressed it
thematically.

Population

In general terms the level of population rose throughout the Highlands
from *c*. 1750 until it reached a peak in the decade 1831–41. It then
declined for the rest of the century. This process has been much
discussed for both cause and consequence. The Highlands came to
be seen, by a number of observers, as overcrowded. This is an issue
in itself because, depending upon one's perspective, emigration and
clearance are either the sad resolution of an endemic problem or an
indefensible tragedy.

Arisaig and Morar shared in the general process but offer their
own individual and harrowing stories. Figure 11 gives the information
we can extract from the various assessments of population in the
district. The evidence for emigration and clearance is set out in Figure
12. This comes primarily from the Statistical Accounts, Census
Returns, the Royal Commissions and surviving passenger-lists of
emigrant ships.

Facts and figures are important, particularly when they are

Figure 11. Population Statistics: North Morar; South Morar and Arisaig

Since the two areas were in different parishes, and belonged to different proprietors, I have separated the figures.

Year	N Morar							S Morar	and	Arisaig				Source
	Houses	Ave House	Males	Females	%F	Age <20 %	Total	S Morar Families	Ave family	Males	Females	Age <20 %	Total	
1764							409						1057	Bishop Hugh Macdonald
1760/5							430							RW Munro
1765													864	OSA (Walker)
1774													1109	SSPCK
1783							460							Rev Reg MacDonell
1793/5							461	243	5.3	579	699	48.6	1278	OSA
1841	83	6.3	253	268	51.4	50.5	521						1219	Census
1851	92	5.9	261	283	52.0	46.0	544						1125	Census
1861	84	5.6	222	247	52.7	43.9	469						1130	Census
1871	84	5.2	217	223	50.7	44.8	440						926	Census
1881	86	5.6	247	238	49.1	48.0	485						909	Census
1891	83	5.3	222	222	50.0	46.8	444						764	Census

a) A comparison of Webster's figures for Ardnamurchan and Glenelg (1755) with surveys done in 1764 and 1774 suggests that he included N. Morar in Ardnamurchan rather than Glenelg. He gives 2300 as the number of Papists in Ardnamurchan parish. Since Ardnamurchan proper and Sunart were almost entirely Protestant whilst Moidart, Arisaig and Morar were almost entirely Catholic, we can assume the figure of 2300 represents these latter three districts. At about 400 for the population of North Morar this gives c. 1100 for Arisaig/South Morar and c. 800 for Moidart, which is consistent with the other evidence we have.

b) In 1774 the population of Arisaig was 828, South Morar was 281 and Moidart was 860.

c) In the Census Returns of 1801-31 the population of Moidart, Arisaig and South Morar was 2165 (1801), 2324 (1811), 2333 (1821) and 2358 (1831). In 1793/5 the population of Arisaig and South Morar was 1278; Moidart was 712. In 1841 the population of Arisaig and South Morar was 1219. Against a background of rising population levels punctuated by emigration and clearance these figures are consistent.

summoned to support a policy. Nigel Mackenzie, Solicitor and Factor
on the Estate of Arisaig, gave evidence to the Napier Commission:

Q. You state that the population of Arisaig was 727, and that it is
    not decreasing?

A. *Not decreasing; it is pretty stationary, according to the census
    tables.*

A glance at Figure 11 will show that Mr Mackenzie was being
economical with the truth – even allowing for the fact that he may
have defined Arisaig more narrowly. Since 1841 the population of
Arisaig and South Morar had declined by up to 40%.

It is impossible to talk about the Clearances or emigration without

Figure 12. Clearance in Arisaig
(Evidence taken from the Deer Forest Commission, 1894)

Location	Tenants evicted	Date
Aird-nam-fuaran	16	c. 1823
Gaoideal	10	1829
Sandaig	1	1829
Doire-na-drise	5	c. 1843
Dubh-chamus	3	c. 1843
Rumach	20	c. 1843
Ardghasaraic	2	c. 1843
Ach-a'-gharbh-uilt	3	c. 1843
Drimindarrach	3	c. 1857
Na Puirt	3	c. 1854
+ 29 cottar families		
Polnish	3	c. 1838
Camus-a'-fhraoich	3	1851
Earna-poll	3	
Ceann-loch-nan-Uamh	3	
Keppoch (including 3 from Poll-Thronndainn)	5	1836
Kinloid (relet to 16 c. 1848)	10	1843
Kinloid	16	c. 1854

The Old Statistical Account claims that, in 1790 and 1791, 322 emigrated
to America. In addition, 11 families moved to the Lowlands between 1780
and 1795.

Fraser-Mackintosh claims that when the Camerons of Fassifern acquired
Meoble they cleared 54 people between Loch Beoraid and Oban.

dealing with the issue of what constitutes over-population. In a rural economy, over-population must be defined in terms of what the local agricultural base can support. In the absence of subsidy, in the absence of mineral or natural resources, in the absence of industry or a failure of trade, can the local farms feed the people? With the rise in population from the mid-eighteenth century the answer in much of the Highland area has been 'No'. As the Highlands became integrated with the rest of Britain, so starvation, which in all previous history had acted as a ruthless check, became unacceptable. Equally unacceptable was the ancient practice of theft. Rising living standards throughout Britain, coupled with rising expectations in the Highlands, created an impossible dilemma. The problem has been wrestled with ever since.

Distribution

Not only did population levels change but the distribution altered. Most of the settlements along the shores of Loch Nevis, Loch Morar and Loch nan Uamh have been deserted. Ardnish, Rhu and the area around Loch an Nostarie have also been abandoned. Distribution today is closely linked to the transport network. This relationship is part cause, part consequence. Where there are groups of people there are demands for roads and better communications. Where there are no roads there are social and economic pressures against people. What we have now is a form of ribbon development along the line of road and railway. The critical factor today is not access by boat, as it has been for all previous history, but access by road. This transformation is very recent. It started at the beginning of the nineteenth century with the building of the first road from Fort William to Arisaig. The pattern of development was confirmed by the line of the railway at the beginning of the twentieth century. Effectively the local population has been redistributed since.

Emigration and Clearance

Emigration from the Highlands has been going on for so long that it has its own history. In Arisaig and Morar it has been recorded from the 1770s. Except for the occasional individual or family, it probably did not take place before this. Problems of over-population were solved within a Highland context, either by starvation or predation.

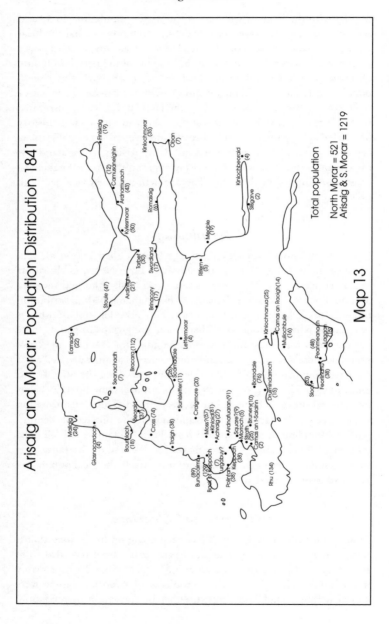

Arisaig and Morar: Population Distribution 1841

Earnsaig (22)
Glaonangardoch (4)
Seanachadh (7)
Mallaig (24)
Bourblach (18)
Feorlig (33)
Cross (74)
Brocara (112)
Traigh (38)
Craigmore (20)
Sunisletter (11)
Scamadale (20)
Lettermorar (4)
Buns Camas (89)
Bracara na Clapoch (12)
Ardnafuaran (91)
Moss?(57)
Kinloid(81)
Achariag (27)
Palinbain (38)
Lurgdbuy?
Key (38)
Square?(9)
Montroch (6)
Brunery(10)
Camas an t-Salainn (2)
Strath (25)
Stoule (47)
Ardnish (21)
Brinacory (17)
Swordland (11)
Torbet (36)
Kylesmorar (50)
Ardmamurach (43)
Camusdheighin (12)
Finisaig (19)
Kinlochmorar (36)
Oban (7)
Romasaig (6)
Meoble (19)
Rifern (5)
Kinlochbeoraid (4)
Silligarve (2)
Borrodale (76)
Druimindarroch (15)
Rhu (134)
Kinlochmanua (25)
Camas an Raoigh (14)
Mullochbuie (16)
Peanmeanach (48)
Feorlindhu (38)
Sloch (6)

Total population

North Morar = 521
Arisaig & S. Morar = 1219

Map 13

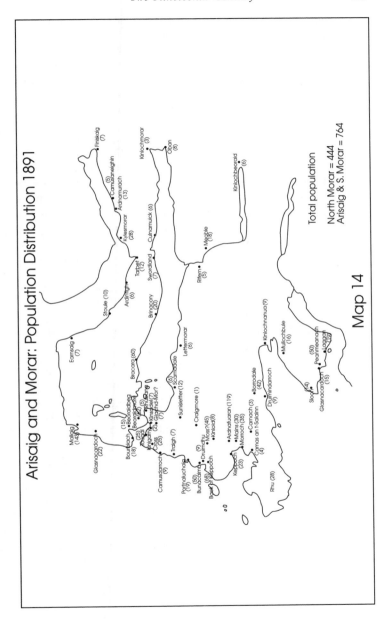

Arisaig and Morar: Population Distribution 1891

Total population

North Morar = 444
Arisaig & S. Morar = 764

Map 14

Finiskaig (7)
Kinlochmorar (3)
Oban (8)
Camusrianach (5)
Ardnamurach (13)
Kylesmorar (28)
Culnamuick (6)
Kinlochbeoraid (6)
Stoule (10)
Ardintigh (6)
Tarbet (12)
Swordland (9)
Brinagory (20)
Meoble (18)
Rifern (5)
Leitirmorar (6)
Earnsaig (7)
Bracara (60)
Scamadale (6)
Kinlochnanua (9)
Mallaig (143)
Sunisletter (12)
Mullochbuie (16)
Glasnacardoch (22)
Beoraidbeg (15)
Beoraidmore (26)
Kinsadel (7)
Gleann-Mor? (22)
Craigmore (1)
Peanmeanach (50)
Smirisary Rhu Arnish (6)
Bourback (18)
Ardnafuaran (119)
Stoul (4)
Glasnacardoch (15)
Glas (28)
Traigh (7)
Mains (30)
Camusdarroch (7)
Drumindarroch (9)
Borrodale (42)
Portnaluchaig (10)
Drumindarroch (9)
Bunacaimb (50)
Morroch (35)
Moss? (45)
Camas an t-Salainn (4)
Kinlokd (8)
Carnoch (3)
Beasdale (8)
Druimindarroch (9)
Kelsopoch (?)
Keppoch (23)
Rhu (28)

Highlanders, over many centuries, earned an unenviable reputation
for stealing: from other clans, from the Lowlands or from Ireland.
They even ventured as far afield as the Northern Isles. There was of
course a cultural overlay to this. It allowed the young men to display
their manliness, their warlike spirit, impress their sweethearts, uphold
an ancestral superiority etc. The prime reason was probably always
economic. The rural economy of the Highlands was so marginal that,
in a bad year, you either stole or starved.

Continued residence is always related to economic opportunity,
even today. Every individual applies this condition to his own circumstances; although from the twentieth century the issue has been
clouded by public subsidy, whether in terms of unemployment benefit
or funding for local enterprise. We stay or migrate depending on the
economic opportunities available to us. In the Highlands there has
always been a restricted range of economic opportunity, which is why
emigration continues. We cannot argue with individuals who decide
to leave. We are less acquiescent when the pressure comes from
landlord or government.

In the nineteenth century the welfare state did not exist and
economic factors applied more harshly. In both Morar and Arisaig
there were estate regulations which we would now regard as wholly
unacceptable. Even at the time they caused moral and religious
condemnation. For North Morar:

> Another strict rule on the Lovat estates may be here mentioned,
> that no squatting is allowed, any crofter taking any family to
> live on his croft beyond his own, being served with notice of
> removal at the first term; nor can any of his own family marry
> and remain on the croft, except the eldest son, if his parents are
> aged and require assistance.
>
> John Peter, Factor for the Lovat Estates, to the Napier
> Commission, 1883

At the same time there was widespread concern in Arisaig over a
recently issued set of estate regulations nicknamed 'The Seventeen
Commandments':

Q. Do you approve of this stipulation that any member of a family
    on attaining twenty-one years of age, whether married or not, is
    bound to find accommodation elsewhere unless allowed to
    remain with the written sanction of the proprietor?

A. *No man is pleased with that stipulation; it is a hard thing for any man to rear a family and expel them when they are twenty-one years of age. It is the young people who support the old. That one is so bad that it almost compels the father to curse his son, and send him out of his house, saying, 'Walk out with you, and let me see your face no more', when the son arrives at the age of twenty-one.*

Donald M'Donald and John M'Eachran, Back of Keppoch,
to Napier Commission, Arisaig, 1883

Attitudes to the Clearances and Emigration can differ radically. With so much of the Highlands now desolate, our response is clouded and confused by emotion. Judgements can be one-sided or incomplete. Contemporaries faced the same dilemmas and often tried to get a spiritual handle on events they could scarcely comprehend.

Clearance evokes shock, grief and anger. Blame is clear and simple. People were evicted; factors, agents, landowners were guilty of cruelty, callousness, even barbarity. There was clearance in Arisaig (see Figure 12). There seems to have been nothing quite comparable in North Morar although oppressive regulation surely drove people out.

Emigration invites sorrow and nostalgia. The issue of blame is sidelined; fatalism and resignation cloud the issue of responsibility. There is a recognition that emigration is an inescapable fact of life if you live in a harsh environment with a marginal economy. Moreover this process continues throughout the Highland area. We cannot blame the young people when they want to leave, to experience the bright lights, the big city. Opportunities for their skills and talents may not exist locally; they may have wider aspirations for themselves and their children. They may simply want to complete their education.

It is always sad to see an area decline, but in a democracy we will never accept social planning of the sort that would make people stay, or choose who is allowed to come in. It is this process which is ongoing, which is currently transforming the Highlands and Highland culture, possibly in the biggest way since the arrival of the Norse a millennium ago.

Homogeneity

One of the clearest things to emerge from a study of the Census Returns is how extraordinarily homogeneous society was. The component questions in each Census give us datasets for forename, surname, housing, occupation, language and birthplace. People shared a few Christian names and surnames; they were born locally and married other locals. There were very few incomers, a fact that is confirmed by the Old Statistical Account for Arisaig in 1795. By 1891 changes in the social fabric were beginning to appear, although it was still largely intact. It was the mobility and commerce and intermarriage of the twentieth century that would change everything.

The Agricultural base

In 1836 Rev Alexander Beith wrote of the parish of Glenelg:

> such quantities of rain fall, and at all seasons, that an agriculturalist might calculate on losing almost every fourth crop. This, and the small comparative amount of arable land, plainly point it out as adapted for pasture, ... sheep pasture, too, principally; as the arable land could not afford sufficient supply of winter provender for any other description of stock.
>
> Besides the tacksmen ... and the shepherds and servants whom they require, the population consists of those who dwell in villages near the sea; – divided into two classes, – such as possess from one acre, to perhaps six of arable ground, and the grazing of from one to three cows, and others who have nothing but the cottage that shelters them, who depend on the kindness of neighbours for patches of ground for potatoes, and supply all their other wants by fishing, and such work as they may obtain at home or abroad.
>
> Rev Alexander Beith, New Statistical Account for Glenelg,
> 1836

Desperation meant that every patch of land was cultivated:

> Sometimes land on the steep sides of hills is seen diligently cultivated by the small tenants, which certainly no capitalist, from motives of profit, would crop; ... this arises from the crowded state of the population in localities not naturally adapted for agriculture, and the necessity, in the absence of better employment, of raising some crop at any rate.
>
> Rev Angus M'Lean, New Statistical Account, Ardnamurchan,
> 1838

Rev Beith produced a little table of the value of local produce. Grain accounted for about 9% (and probably an even lower proportion in North Morar), potatoes about 6%, pasture of cattle and sheep about 74%, herring about 2%. The herring fishery was only worth about £250 a year to locals and yet in 1882, according to the proprietor of Knoydart, Loch Hourn produced something like £180,000 worth of herring. In Figure 13 I have made some comparisons across the local area. It is clear that farming was still the mainstay of the local economy well into the nineteenth century, long after it had proved inadequate.

According to George Taylor, North Morar was slow to switch to sheep-farming:

> Sheep farming having been, but to a limited extent, introduced into North Morar, a greater extent of soil, in proportion to the population, is under tillage than in the other Districts of the Parish. The means of subsistence are, therefore, generally more abundant, and ignorance less prevalent, than in many of the surrounding Districts.
>
> North Morar Enumeration, 1841 Census Return

The nineteenth century saw the continued decline of agriculture as the cornerstone of the Highland economy. In 1748 livestock, principally cattle, but also some sheep, horses and goats, paid the rent, while grain crops provided only a small proportion of their annual needs. By 1798 the local economy in Arisaig was becoming increasingly

Figure 13. Table of Produce – Arisaig and Morar

| | Arisaig and South Morar (1795) | | Glenelg (1836) | |
	Value in £	%	Value in £	%
Grain	317	4	1000	9
Potatoes	550	8	650	6
Hay, stock and pasture	6194.5	87	8485	80
Gardens and orchards	10		50	
Woods	66		200	2
Fish/herring	70	1	250	2

North Morar is the poorest and least fertile part of Glenelg parish.

Figures drawn from the Old Statistical Account (Ardnamurchan parish) and New Statistical Account (Glenelg parish). I have combined some of the component units in order to make comparisons.

dependent on kelp production, while potatoes were replacing grain crops. Cattle, which for centuries had sustained a droving trade, were yearly failing before sheep. James Hogg, the 'Ettrick Shepherd', who knew about sheep-farming, made the following observations when he visited Arisaig:

> The country hereabouts had a more promising appearance than the banks of Loch-Moidart; the hills were moderately high, and towards the coast low, and mixed with spots of arable ground, not unfertile, altho' badly tilled, and their ridges formed after the pattern of the new moon. In all these districts the sheep stocks were well attended to, and the breeds were, on many farms, above mediocrity: they are all of the blackfaced breeds, and some of the smaller farmer's stocks retain too striking marks of their consanguinity to the old degenerate highland breed. Smearing with tar and grease is becoming more general, but even those which we saw unsmeared were not much ragged in their fleeces: the frost there is never very intense, when the salt-impregnated vapours are unfavourable to the breeding of vermin upon them. There are likewise large herds of black cattle, but amongst the better sort of farmers or tacksmen, these are yearly losing ground.

The problem was that the sheep were usually owned by large-scale graziers who had no wish to share the hillside with people. They could also offer much higher rents to the landowner.

By the time of the potato famine in 1846–7 the local population had become completely dependent upon potatoes. In the immediate aftermath of the blight some grain crops were sown again, but by 1883 these were only a distant memory:

> We have made no meal for the last thirty years. [i.e. grown no oats for oatmeal] ...
>
> Donald M'Donald and John M'Eachran, Back of Keppoch, to
> Napier Commission, 1883

Monoculture had spelt disaster at the time of the 1846 potato blight. Robert Somers visited Arisaig the following year:

> I went ashore on the north side of the bay, and directed my steps to a solitary cottage, the inmate of which came to the door to inquire my errand, ... I learned that he was a woollen weaver,

very ill employed, worse paid, and in much distress. I was asked at length to step into the interior of the cottage. At one end stood the loom, and at the other a fire of brushwood burned weakly on the earthen floor. A deal-board resting upon a few large stones, and serving the purposes of a bed, and a dresser containing a few bowls and plates, formed the only furniture of the apartment. The floor was very cleanly swept, and the poor man's wife had evidently done everything in her power to make things comfortable; but the bare stone walls, and the large smoke-hole in the roof, through which the wind swirled in cold draughts, gave the house a very desolate appearance. This family had a cow, but the pressure of the famine compelled them to part with her ...

Somers' comments help to explain the tenacity with which Highlanders clung to their land. It was a form of security in a marginal economy:

I have found everywhere in the Highlands that tradesmen are the most destitute class of the population. Where the mass of the people are so poor, food is the only necessary of life. Shoes and articles of clothing are luxuries; and when a pinch comes, the tailor, the shoemaker, and the weaver, are the first to find no demand for their labour. This poor weaver showed me a piece of cloth which had remained with him all summer, because the owner was too poor to pay him for his work upon it.

Prospects were bleak, whilst the scourge of absentee landlordism meant complete dissociation between proprietor and tenant:

Formerly nothing but potatoes were grown, and a planting of six barrels has been known to yield as many as a hundred. This last season corn was grown instead, and a return of four or five bolls of meal is all which most of the crofters have to maintain their families upon till another harvest ... The forty families who have no land are perpetually in destitution; and the crofters will be equally wretched as soon as their two or three months' supply of meal is exhausted. There is no work whatever going on upon the estate. Lord Cranstoun and his factor are both absentees. The one lifts the rent, and the other carries it off and consumes it; and this comprehends the whole of the relation between landlord and tenant in Arisaig.

Somers, like so many others, was appalled at the moral injustice, at the gulf between rich and poor. In truth this has always been part of Highland history; what is new is that from the nineteenth century we have been less prepared to condone it:

> Arisaig, with its £1,200 a-year, was a windfall to Lord Cranstoun, an unexpected addition to his wealth, for which he never toiled, nor lost a sixpence ... He regarded his Highland estate as simply entitling him to a wider round of pleasure; and in the fashionable saloons of London this English nobleman has squandered in a few hours of luxury, ... the hundreds which cost the poor people of Arisaig a year of toil and privation to collect.
>
> R Somers, *Letters from the Highlands*, 1848

There are rich and poor in many parts of Britain. It is just that in the Highlands the contrasts are very sharp, and history casts a longer shadow.

It is ironic that at the very moment when crofting was about to achieve secure legal status, the evidence given to the Napier Commission in Arisaig indicated that crofting could not possibly answer the people's needs:

> The stirks on an average do not pay our rents, and if our main dependence, namely the herring fishing, proves a failure, we must have recourse to whelk gathering to aid us in paying our rents, as for the last eight years we have had no work provided by the proprietor ...
>
> Q. So that you have to live entirely by the profits of your own crofts?
> A. *We could not live by that; we are dependent upon the herring fishing, and if it fails we have recourse to the whelk gathering.*
>
> Colin and Ranald Macdonald, Bunacaimb, to Napier
> Commission, 1883

In general terms the kelp industry collapsed after the Napoleonic wars whilst cattle droving went into long decline. Sheep swept all before them until the last quarter of the nineteenth century when much of the Highlands was transformed into deer forest. Neither sheep nor deer require much human labour. Locals grew increasingly dependent upon the proprietor for support, eking out a pittance from the soil, the sea and the shore.

The following extracts from the Napier Commission Report illustrate the dilemmas faced by local people. There was moral indignation at clearance, a recognition that crofting could not support them, and yet an extraordinary attachment to the land. There was dependence upon the proprietor for work, a sense of injustice and a sense of realism.

Firstly there was grievance at deprivation of land. This made people completely dependent upon the proprietor for work:

> The Strath, or village, of Arisaig contains about twenty-six families of very poor people. It has grievances of its own – such as utter landlessness, excessive rents, and want of constant employment. People do not expect any one to give employment for the mere sake of the labourers; but these people urge that the families to which many of them belonged were turned out of the better lands where they could employ themselves; and that, thus, they have a moral right to constant employment at good wages ...

Q. Was it about eight years ago that work ceased to be given to you in this Strath?

A. *Yes, chiefly after the death of old Mr Astley.*

Q. Before that time were you in steady employment?

A. *Yes, indeed.*

Q. And were you paid reasonable wages?

A. *Yes; very fair.*

Q. And you were able to live in some comfort then, at least those who lost the land?

A. *Very good ...*

Q. If you got the choice of a good croft in one of these places, or steady employment as you had before Mr Astley's death, which would you prefer?

A. *(M'Eachran). I would prefer the land.*

Q. Have you tried both ways?

A. *We have tried both ...*

Q. And, having tried both ways, would you still prefer the croft?

A. *I would rather the croft than anything.*

Alexander M'Pherson (assisted by Alexander M'Eachran),
Strath, Napier Commission, 1883

There was the aspiration:

> What we wish done for us is that we will get the land we at
> present possess at its real value, that the rent be fixed by land
> commissioners appointed by Government, or that the land be
> otherwise fairly valued, that all the land which was taken from
> our township be restored, and that we be not removed so long
> as we pay a fair rent. Seeing that our forefathers have been here
> from time immemorial, we consider that we have as much right
> to live in comfort here as the proprietor has to be superior over
> us. As to emigration – what land has a greater right to sustain
> us than the land for which our forefathers suffered and bled?
> Why should we emigrate? There is plenty of waste land around
> us; for what is an extensive deer forest in the heart of the most
> fertile part of our land but waste land? ... The deer forest itself,
> once land flowing with milk and honey, which supported scores
> of families in comfort, but who, alas! are now, on the account
> of the mania for sport scattered over the wide world, is far better
> than all the land now cultivated by the poor crofters.
>
>   Donald M'Donald and John M'Eachran, Back of Keppoch,
>   Napier Commission, 1883

There was indignation at the way people could treat each other.
Rev Donald MacCallum, Minister of Arisaig, discusses the recent
death of Mary O'Henly or M'Donald, reputedly of starvation:

> We are not concerned to prove that the woman died of starvation,
> but ... the case goes, along with other things, to show the kind
> of feeling with which the people on the estate are regarded. If,
> instead of a human being dying of starvation, it had been the
> killing of a deer or the spearing of a salmon, that had become
> a matter of public concern. It would not have been allowed to
> lie over, as the case of Mary O'Henly has done.
>
>   Napier Commission, Arisaig, 1883

His accusation rings true. The Highlands were being turned into a
playground for the rich, and the rich would protect their investment
and their sport whatever the social consequences. Sheep-farming
became less profitable in the last quarter of the nineteenth century.
Deer forests offered much better returns to the landowner. The hidden
costs of deer were largely borne by the poorer residents who struggled

to protect their crops. As Donald M'Donald, Polnish, said to the Deer Forest Commission:

Our demands are not great. We would be thankful for as much land as would afford us summering and wintering for a cow, and land in which we could plant a few potatoes; and we wish to be protected from the deer above all things. Sheep were bad enough, but the deer have nearly finished us.

At the heart of the problem was a changed relationship between landlord and tenant. The levers of economic power were now wholly in the hands of the landowner. In mediaeval times, chiefs could not extract much money rental from their clansmen. Might was the number of fighting men you could raise. Now money was power, and fairness is a concept alien to economic relationships. In the long run most landlords were simply interested in the most rent.

Mr Mackenzie, the Factor on the Arisaig Estate:

I know that the proprietrix of this estate is exceedingly anxious to satisfy every aspiration which she considers reasonable.

Q. But she reserves to herself the right of saying what is reasonable and what is not on the part of the crofters?
A. *Naturally.*

Napier Commission, Arisaig, 1883

There was a sense in some districts that the problem was not of their own making:

the present overcrowding is not from rapid multiplication nor from wilful subdivision. The crowding and the poverty are the result of the clearing of the townships of Goadal and Ardna-fuaran, which are now partly in the possession of two tacksmen and partly in the possession of a sportsman, and under deer. Besides those who were put in among us, as mentioned great numbers were obliged to emigrate, and the numbers who are crowded together on the bad and small lots, and on no lots at all, are no indication of the extent of land which lies in a state of comparative waste under the sheep and deer and cattle of the few. The truth is that the greater part of this estate is in the hands of three tacksmen, besides some held by the proprietor; and an extensive deer forest, which could support many families in comfort ... we confess here that many a time we could not live at all but from the shell-fish from the sea-shore ... Our best source of income is shell-fish ...

Donald M'Varish, Ardnish, Napier Commission, 1883

At this point Donald makes an unfortunate admission:

Q. Do men gather whelks as well as women and children?
A. *Yes, but it is very hard work for the men.*

Q. Is it not harder for the women and children?
A. *They don't complain of it so much.*

Ibid

Clearance had dire social and psychological effects – as described by Aeneas Macdonell of Camusdarrach:

In Lord Cranstoun's time the first clearances commenced in this country, and I was then a young boy almost; but I shall never forget the feelings of awe and fear that came over the people of the country when the last occurred ... from my recollection of the people long ago in my boyhood, I should say that the old people were a finer race, I mean the fathers and grandfathers of these here. They were fine-looking men, and men of a very independent noble spirit, who were on the most cordial and friendly terms with their chiefs; at that time it was Clanranald, ... They looked upon their chief as their father, and had no feeling of fear or awe such as they have of proprietors now-a-days.

Aeneas Macdonell, Camusdarrach, Napier Commission, 1883

But could crofting ever support the local population? In 1883, Rev Charles Macdonald, Moidart, gave evidence as to what Lord Howard, owner of the Moidart estate, regarded as the desirable size of croft:

He thinks it is almost impossible to put tenants in a decent, comfortable, and respectable way, and in a way that would make them independent, more or less, of any extra labour or employment from the estate, without eight or twelve acres of arable ground and about six cows with their followers ... And ... about fifty sheep.

Rev Charles Macdonald, Moidart, Napier Commission, 1883

In 1894 Mr Mackay spoke to the Deer Forest Commission on the subject of the minimum size of croft in Knoydart. He stated that in order to live 'pretty fairly', a crofter 'should have at least twenty acres of arable land'.

What populations could such estimates support? In 1834 Boulton calculated that there were 534 (Scots) acres of arable land in North Morar (although it is unlikely that any modern land surveyor would arrive at anything like such a generous assessment). However, if we accept Boulton's figure and set the minimum requirement at 12 acres of arable, then North Morar could have carried some 45 crofters. In 1891 the average household size in North Morar was 5.3, which would mean that a crofting base could support no more than about 240 people. The actual population was 444. In 1841, before the fishing industry developed in Mallaig, it had been 521. Agriculture, as the basis of the Highland economy, had failed long before either of the Royal Commissions.

This is confirmed by exchanges before the Deer Forest Commission. Mr Nicholson, husband of the owner of the Arisaig estate, was able to cross-question other witnesses before giving evidence himself. As was to be expected, he argued the landowner's case. His views were those of contemporary laissez-faire capitalism. The problem is that they resonate today just as they did then. We may have no sympathy for landowners, but in a democracy there are always going to be differing views about social intervention. Put bluntly, should the city subsidise the country? Do the rural poor have any greater moral claim than the urban poor? Is the croft more deserving than the ghetto?

Arisaig men were unusually realistic in their expectations. They wanted more land, but they did not expect crofting to be able to support them. In the context of the evidence given to the Commission elsewhere, this was exceptional. The problem was that if the landowner did not employ them, there was little other work available. As Mr Nicholson said:

> The present crofters, having had their rents fixed by the Crofters Commission, tell me that the crofts do not pay, and that there is not labour enough in the place for them to make a good livelihood, and I don't see how you are going to improve their position.

And of cottars (i.e. those without land):

> ... their case is that of the poorer persons in any town, in Fort William, or in Glasgow, who have no land. If they cannot make

their living out of their labour, like people of other places, they
must go somewhere else.

A W Nicholson to the Deer Forest Commission, Arisaig,
21 August 1894

When challenged that current economic practice might lead to the
complete depopulation of parts of the Highlands, Mr Nicholson said:

my own view, sorry though I should be personally to see persons
who are attached to the place, and who have lived on it all their
lives, go away, is that they should not be treated differently from
any other class in the community, whether my own class or any
other, if the force of circumstances is hard upon them.

These political and economic dilemmas trouble us still.

Fishing

Yet in the midst of all this decline the seeds of future prosperity had
been sown. The evidence of Boulton's map of North Morar (See Plate
14) suggests that, even before the potato blight, Lord Lovat had
planned a wholesale shift in economic policy. The evidence presented
in the last chapter shows that as late as the 1830s most families fished
only to satisfy their own needs. Boulton's map dates from 1834 and
suggests that Lovat was already planning to resettle some of his
tenants and create a fishing community in Mallaig.

The process becomes visible in the Census Returns. In 1841 only
three men in North Morar list their occupation as 'Fisher'; by 1851
this has risen to 31; by 1891 to 56, which accounted for over one-third
of adult male employment. The village of Mallaig seems to have
become fully established in the decade 1841–51 when the population
grew from 24 to 134. Lovat and his agents must have foreseen that
an agricultural base for the local economy was no longer sufficient.
With the potato famine providing further stimulus, Lovat paid for
some of the necessary infrastructure:

In addition to the reclaiming the ground by the late Lord Lovat
in 1846 and 1847, a large outlay was also incurred at that time
by his Lordship in making roads and a pier at Mallaig.

John Peter, Napier Commission, 1883

Although Mallaig became the biggest community in North Morar, it remains true that in 1891 the majority of local fishermen lived elsewhere. They are found scattered through the tiny communities on the south side of Loch Nevis and even on Loch Morar-side. The local fishing industry was still relatively small-scale and under-capitalised. Lots of small boats fished close to home and primarily in certain seasons of the year. Moreover, while more people became fishermen, there is little evidence in the Census returns for any corresponding growth in ancillary trades such as coopering or boat-building.

The local fishing industry was extremely volatile in the nineteenth century. There were good years and bad years. Access to markets was a crucial factor and it was the building of the railway line which secured this uncertain investment. Guaranteed quick access to markets throughout Britain ensured a bright future for Mallaig in the twentieth century. The village expanded, businesses and trades grew with the fishing, people drifted there from the other communities. The population of North Morar has more than doubled since its high point in 1851. In terms of the depopulation and decline experienced elsewhere in the Highlands, this is quite exceptional.

In the context of recent developments in fish-farming, and fish conservation, Captain Swinburne, RN, appears unusually prescient. He was proprietor of Eilean Shona, Moidart, and made strenuous efforts to develop a local fishing industry:

> I think also that the oysters and mussels would be a great source of wealth and employment in this country. There are lochs all over the west coast, with a very fine climate, where oysters are to be found, to a certain extent, and mussels; but they are not looked after or cultivated ... There are miles of the sea coast fitted for oyster and mussel cultivation ...

> When I came here at first I used to work the lobster industry; but I found that the supply was falling off. There is a Scottish law which forbids fishing between certain dates; I stuck to the law, while others fished all the year round, especially in the summer time, and that, I think, should be prevented. In a few years there will be no lobsters at all.

> Q. (Lord Napier). We ate two lobsters today?
> A. *Then you are lucky; in a few years you will not.*
>
> Q. Ought this present time to be made a close time?
> A. *Yes, I think it should.*

Q.   (Professor Mackinnon). The law makes the close time from
      the 1st of June to the 1st of September?
A.   *Yes.*

Q.   But it is never observed?
A.   *No, I don't think it is.*

                              Napier Commission, Arisaig, 6 August 1883

It is not recorded whether members of the Commission, – a lord, a
baronet, two MPs, a professor and a sheriff – suffered any form of
indigestion from the close-season lobsters they enjoyed in Arisaig in
August 1883.

Transport

The very beginning of the nineteenth century saw a development
which, perhaps more than any other, secured the economic future of
Arisaig and Morar. This was the building of the road from Fort
William to Arisaig, which, over subsequent years, was gradually
extended north to Mallaig. In 1800 the government had set up a
Commission for Roads and Bridges in the Highlands. It was intended
to relieve some of the economic and structural problems of the area
by providing half the cost of new roads and bridges. The very first
road to be started under this scheme was what became known as the
'Loch na Gaul' road between Fort William and Arisaig. This has been
ably dealt with by A R B Haldane in his book *New Ways through
the Glens*. Although not complete until 1812, this road transformed
the economic potential of the area.

Stretches of the old road can still be seen on the way up the Muidhe
and just at the eastern entrance to the railway tunnel at Beasdale.
This latter is particularly impressive. The wayside is now thickly
wooded but the line of the road is clearly visible and some of the
stone culverts are still intact. However, it should not perhaps be
viewed as a completely fresh start. Cattle-droving from the Highlands
was a long-established industry and a well-worn track may already
have existed. Writing in 1804, when work on the 'Loch na Gaul' road
was only just beginning, James Hogg says:

This road by which we had come from Arisaig is all tolerably
good, saving about three miles in the middle, which is nearly
impassible; and as it is much the nearest communication betwixt

the south country and the extensive and populous isles in the shires of Inverness and Ross, the rendering of it a safe and easy passage for horses and carriages, is certainly a matter of much national utility.

A Journey Through the Highlands and Western Isles, in the Summer of 1804.

This evidence is reinforced by John MacCulloch:

Every one who can find time or make it, should bestow a day on an excursion from Fort William to Arasaik. It is a beautiful ride of forty miles. As to the road itself, it is, like all the new ones which are so little used, ... more like a gravel walk in a garden, than a highway ... It is a great pleasure, unquestionably, to see and to use such roads as these; but it would be much more pleasing to find them cut up, or, at least, marked by wheel tracks and hoof marks; that we might have the satisfaction of knowing that they were used, and that some interchange of something, if it was but that of ideas, was going on in this country ...

it is impossible to give too much praise to the ingenuity which conducted this, as well as some other of these Highland roads ... In many cases, the new roads have been traced, along, or very near to, the ancient cattle and country tracks; ... in many more, the distribution is due to the common Highlanders themselves, sometimes contractors, and sometimes overseers; ... I, for one, will lift up my voice, ... in defence of the talents and ingenuity of these Highland workmen: among the lowest of whom I have found such an eye for ground, and such a quick conception of its height, and distribution, and inclination, ... as even a general officer or a quarter-master might often envy. They are natural geographers ...

These roads are, however, very treacherous, in spite of all the care bestowed on them: for, against torrents, it is often impossible to calculate, and, even when foreseen, they are sometimes not to be resisted ... This very road was in perfect repair when I passed it first. When I returned in a few days, a foundation wall had slid away from a steep face of smooth rock, and the road was gone.

The Highlands and Western Isles of Scotland, 1824

The road seems to have been gradually extended northwards, and a bridge over the River Morar appears on Boulton's map of 1834. In the two centuries since, the line of the road has only been modified although the question of improving or upgrading it has become something of a local political issue. There are also minor roads along the north side of Rhu to the old steamer pier and along the north shore of Loch Morar to Bracorina. At Bracorina it continues as a bridle path to Tarbet on Loch Nevis.

There are other examples of early civil engineering projects in the area. There is an impressive set of stepping stones across Lochan Stole on the hill-path between Bracorina and Stoul. There are the stone piers of an old bridge across Allt an Loin. They offer a glimpse of vanished communities with very practical requirements.

Although, with hindsight, the building of the road seems to have been critical for the future economic welfare of the district, it was less obvious at the time. Rev Angus M'Lean, writing for the New Statistical Account in 1838, states that cattle and sheep were driven to southern markets via the Loch-na-Gaul road:

> The steam communication is, however, chiefly adopted by travellers of all descriptions. By the Glasgow steamers, to which access is had at ... the point of Arasaig, some cattle and sheep, and great quantities of eggs, are sent to the south, and the greater part of the oatmeal, groceries, hard and stone-wares, and other manufactures for the use of the parish imported.

By comparison with the horse and cart, a steamship offered speed and bulk carriage. It was only after the invention of the motor car and lorry that the road came into its own.

Tourism

It is easy to regard tourism as a modern industry. In Arisaig it is nearly two centuries old. We have already seen how, in 1763, there was talk of building a change-house in Arisaig 'for the Entertainment of Strangers and Passengers'.

By June 1804, when James Hogg visited the district, the inn had a good reputation and the Jacobite yarn was already being spun:

> We passed several small islands, on one of which there is a vitrified fort, and we came to the very creek where the unfortunate

Prince Charles Stewart first landed on the mainland of Scotland in the year 1745. Yea, ... the same woman who entertained them still resides on the spot, though now in somewhat of a better house. After again walking over some low hills, we came to a good road, which led us to the village of Arisaig, where there is a good inn, at which we arrived ere it was quite dark, and were comfortably lodged.

Hogg was rightly sceptical of some of the wilder claims already being made in the name of Bonnie Prince Charlie. A few days later he was less fortunate in his choice of lodgings at Kinlochailort:

In a short time, however, the breeze again set in, and bore us safely into Arisaig, where we dined, and that evening travelled to Kinloch-Enort a stage on the road to Fort William.

When we arrived there the people were all in bed, but on rapping loudly at the door, the landlord, a big black, terrible-looking fellow, came stark naked, and let us in: he then lighted a candle, tied on his kilt, and asked how far we had come today. We told him from Harries. He stared us full in the faces, and perceiving that we were in our sober senses, answered only with a hem! as much as to say, I know how you should be believed. He then shewed us into a little damp room with an earthen floor and set before us what cheer he had in the house for supper, which consisted of cakes, milk, and rum, for what is very strange, he had no whisky. In this same apartment there were two heather beds without hangings, on one of which a woman and some children were lying. Mr W. was now in a terrible passion, and swore he would abandon that horrid place, and take shelter in the woods. The woman and children, however, slid away; the beds were made up with clean cloathes, and we were obliged to pass the night on them the best way we could.

Mr L. complained much in the morning of several rude engravings made on his body by the stubborn roots of the heather and Mr G.'s back was all tamboured work but I, by being forced to take to the bed which the family had left, got the advantage of a feather bed among the heath.

Catherine Sinclair in her book *Scotland and the Scotch*, published in 1840, writes of her visit to the inn at Arisaig:

the innkeeper seemed in as much consternation at the arrival of travellers, as if we had ... rode upon broomsticks. Till the landlady recovered her presence of mind, she ushered us into the kitchen, apologising that her parlour and three best bed-rooms had been constantly occupied during the last twelve summers by a trio of gentlemen from Oxford, who come there to enjoy fishing and shooting during the whole season ... Late in the evening, we were at length shown into a sitting-room, resembling an armoury of guns, varied by fishing rods, and adorned with a ... variety of flies.

So people were coming for fishing and shooting holidays in Arisaig at least as early as 1828. It was always important to bear a trophy home, and, if you had not been successful yourself, you could always buy one.

The Bay of Arisaig is a favourite resort of seals. The Highlanders still attribute the common habit of these animals of following boats, to their love of music ... But we had no music for the entertainment of our pursuers but that of a rifle, which was successful in one instance. The animal shot sunk, and floated afterwards ashore ... The price of the skin varies from twelve to twenty-four shillings. The public-house, at the head of the bay, contains a large assortment, for sale, of the skins of seals, wild-cats, pole-cats, and otters.

Lord Teignmouth, *Sketches of the Coasts and Islands of Scotland*, 1836

However, the rich, particularly the nineteenth-century rich, did not often let the interests of other people come between them and their sport. As the century progressed, more and more of the Highlands was turned into deer forest. In our area there were deer forests in Rhu (Arisaig), the eastern half of North Morar, and the Meoble estate in South Morar.

Catherine Sinclair was well aware of another side to life in the Highlands:

Lord Cranstoun's beautifully situated cottage near this ... shows no resemblance to a cottage, except in the name, being a solid substantial square mansion, situated in a perfect paradise for sportsmen, as the grounds are quite a zoological garden of birds, animals, and fish, wild, tame, and amphibious, every species of living creature in short, except mankind ... The motto of Lord Cranstoun's family is rather a selfish one, 'Thou shalt want ere I want!'

Catherine Sinclair, Scotland and the Scotch, 1840

In 1894, Mr Nicholson did see some future in the tourist industry:

Q. Then, do you anticipate that this part of the country might to some extent become a fashionable resort for, – I would not say tourists exactly, but residenters during a certain period of the year?

A. *I take it that we shall see more. Even with the present communications I think that if not every year, every period of five years sees more tourists and people coming to the district; but I must say they come for a very short time in the year.*

Deer Forest Commission, Arisaig, 1894

Like every industry, tourism brings its own problems. The season is still short and unpredictable. Wealthy people from the cities or other countries buy up local property for holiday cottages or part-time residence. The Highlands are not the only part of rural Britain to experience this difficulty, but the population is so fragile that it has an especial impact.

Catching the Ferry!

Throughout Scotland there seem to have been ferry arrangements at popular crossing points from very early times. However these only applied to certain places along the west coast and in the Hebrides. For all other requirements the first travellers just had to hire boats as and when they could.

Mrs Murray, a remarkable stravaiger for her time, describes a voyage north from Bunessan in Mull. Her account is interesting because it sheds light on the dangers inherent in sea-travel among the islands, and because the boat was the property of two men from South Morar:

It was a large flat bottomed boat, made on purpose to transport cattle and sheep from one island to another. There was in it one division for beasts, one for passengers, a hole to cook victuals in, and another hole for the people to lie down in, which latter dark places I did not approach. The boat was navigated by two

south Morair men to whom it belonged, and we set sail from
Bunessain on the 21st of July 1802, at seven o'clock in the
morning, and steered for the island of Eigg.

As the journey progressed, both wind and tide turned against them
and the boat made for Coll instead. However:

all along the coast of Coll there are innumerable rocks in the
sea, some to be seen, others concealed. The boatmen were
unacquainted with the navigation, and began to be out of pa-
tience, and out of humour, declaring that if it became dark before
they arrived at the Loch, at the head of which Coll's house is
built, they would not venture into it, by reason of the numbers
of rocks they had heard (for they were never there) lay scattered
in it. We passed point after point, but no harbour appeared. The
boatmen began to talk loud in Gaelic, and damn in English, for
there is no such oath in the Gaelic language; ... The sea was
dashing, the sails rattling, the sailors hollowing and shouting; in
short, except in the gulf of Coire Vreaikain [Corryvreckan], it
was the greatest bustle I ever was in.

At this point a small fishing boat came up to the cattle-boat and Mrs
Murray hastily transferred herself:

We had not been out of the large boat three minutes, before she
struck upon a rock ... happily however, the boat was quickly
extricated from the rock, and soon after, to my great satisfaction,
safely anchored.

Mrs Murray drew the following conclusion from her disquieting
experience:

All who navigate the sounds between island and island in the
Hebrides, should be careful to have their crew well acquainted
with the harbours and coasts of every island they propose to
visit, for otherwise, should night from unavoidable delays surprise them, they run infinite risks of being lost.

Hon Mrs Murray, *Companion and Useful Guide to the
Beauties of Scotland*, 1805

James Hogg reinforces this warning in his description of a passage
from Irin, on the south shore of Loch Ailort, to the north shore of
Loch nan Uamh in 1804:

We at length reached the genteel house of Ewrin, where we were again entertained by Mr McEchern, who entreated us to stay all night, but perceiving that we wished to get forward, procured us a boat and crew to carry us over. The boat being small, and crouded, and the sea very rough, we were certainly in considerable danger; the waves often washing over her, threatened to suffocate us with brine; the man at the rudder however always bid us fear nothing, and, to encourage us, sung several Earse songs.

Arisaig, and later Mallaig, were important as ferry terminals. In the early days it was not always the case that such services were either regular or punctual. There was also a tendency, on the part of some travel writers, to paint a picture of the Highlander as lazy, disorganised and backward. The travelogue is therefore a good way to view the interface between two cultures which were struggling to understand each other. We can recognise the prejudice – and the humour. John MacCulloch tells us:

> I had been directed to Sky by this route, as the best and the most commodious, and as there was, at Arasaik, the best of all possible ferry boats. But when the enquiry came to be made, nobody knew any thing about a ferry boat. There might be one, or not: if there was, it was uncertain if it would carry a horse; whether it was on this side of the water or the other; whether it would choose to go; whether there was a ferryman; whether the wind would allow it to go; whether the tide would suffer it. The Arasaik road had been made on account of the ferry, or the ferry on account of the road; and though a carriage ferry, and a horse ferry, there was no boat that could hold a carriage, and no horse had ever dared to cross. Furthermore, the ferry-boat, if there really was one, was two miles from Arasaik, somewhere, among some rocks; and there was no road to it, nor any pier. Lastly, I at length found a ferry-boat, a mile from the sea, as fit to carry a camelopardalis as a horse, and a ferry-boat man who could not speak English.

MacCulloch follows this with a long rigmarole about the rival claims of two ferryboats, one blue, one black; the owner of the former: drunk, the owner of the latter: unwilling or missing. Besides, 'there was no one to navigate the vessel but the ferryman's wife, and she was employed in whipping her children'. The saga started on Sunday but by Tuesday MacCulloch was embarked because the ferry had been loaned to some other men whom he managed to persuade to take him:

> In the end, the men admitted me, ... with a promise to land me somewhere in Sky; if they did not change their minds. The horse did as he liked: it is good to conform to all events in this part of the world; and I was thus accommodated ... with a passage to Sky, or elsewhere, in a ferry-boat over which I had no controul: in a ferry-boat which was not a ferry-boat, and which had no ferryman. All the arrangements were of the usual fashion; no floor, no rudder, no seat aft, oars patched and spliced and nailed, no rowlocks, a mast without stay, bolt, or haulyards; and all other things fitting, as the advertisements say.
>
> My companions were soon tired of rowing, and, as usual, would set a sail. As it could not be hoisted, for want of haulyards, the yard was fastened to the mast, and thus it was all set up together, after much flapping and leeway. It was then found that there was neither tack nor sheet; besides which, three or four feet at the after leach were torn away. The holes in the sail were convenient; because they saved the trouble of reefing, in case of a squall ... And then the boat began to go backwards. I did not care; it was a fine day and a long day, and an entertaining coast: they were good-natured fellows, and I was as well at sea as in Sky or Arasaik.

> John MacCulloch, *The Highlands and Western Isles of Scotland*, 1824

This sanguine view of the ferry arrangements in Arisaig is partially endorsed by Lord Teignmouth a few years later:

> At Arisaig there is a ferry to Sky: a species of conveyance very different from that which the Southerns understand by such a mode of proceeding, and implying, in this instance, a transit of fifteen miles, – the delay in preparing the boat, which lies two miles distant from Arisaig, – the catching the boatmen, the clearing the coast, the management of intricate tides and conflicting winds, and the probability of a thorough ducking.

> Lord Teignmouth, *Sketches of the Coasts and Islands of Scotland*, 1836

CHAPTER 9

THE TWENTIETH CENTURY

What were the critical developments of the twentieth century for Arisaig and Morar? The Highlands, like the rest of Britain, have been transformed, but which were those developments that will determine future patterns of employment? Is it traditional industries like agriculture and fishing; is it the new technologies of computing and telecommunications; or will the Highlands become a collection of wildlife and heritage theme parks for the rest of Britain? Where will Arisaig and Morar find their niche in a changing economic environment, within a European framework?

For some of these developments it is still too early to say. The twentieth century has only recently ended. People are naturally conservative and cling to their old habits, customs and ways of making a living. They use political means to sustain the tried and tested economic forms. But nobody can persist for long in uneconomic behaviour unless somebody else is willing to subsidise them. If we look back at the sweeping changes wrought in the twentieth century, which will prove to be the crucial ones?

Agriculture

Agriculture is now of minimal importance in Arisaig and Morar, and this trend seems set to continue. Two World Wars meant that during the twentieth century there was a strategic imperative to grow as much food as possible in Britain. This political determinant long provided an economic cushion for farmers. Domestic food production was encouraged and subsidised.

This approach now seems dead. Wars are more likely to be either global and intense or local and bitter. The long attritional struggles of the First and Second World Wars are unlikely to be repeated. As a result the strategic requirement for home-grown food has disappeared.

This will reflect itself in a permanent change of political attitude towards farmers.

Supermarkets in southern Britain now get their food from every corner of the globe. This even extends to perishable foods like vegetables or shellfish which come straight from Africa or the Americas respectively. How can the Highlands with their poor land, dire weather and short growing season compete with this? They cannot, and we should expect agriculture to play an increasingly marginal role. There may be niche markets which can be developed by far-sighted entrepreneurs; there will be continued support for crofting, but the current trend is away from livestock farming. The mantra now is 'diversification'. This often carries the sub-text – 'out of farming'.

Forestry

In theory, the Highlands offer good growing conditions for timber but forestry is not yet of major importance in Arisaig and Morar. There have been some small-scale schemes in the past and there is currently a project underway by Loch an Nostarie. Forestry, though, is land- rather than labour-intensive. Contracts for fencing, planting and felling are short-lived unless the forest is on a very large scale. Nevertheless forestry has a place, not least because mature woodlands would help to restore the landscape.

Forestry does impose restrictions on the presence and movement of sheep and deer, issues that are not readily faced. In addition there is always going to be some tension between forests as ecologically desirable and trees as a cash crop. We like our woodlands to be visually attractive and varied. We may not like the trees that grow fastest or give the best returns. We do not want them to be all of the same type or planted in straight lines. We may not want them clear-felled. In such ways our prejudices cloud objectives that were formerly just economic. Aesthetics have an unusually high profile in the forestry industry.

Fishing

Fishing has unquestionably been the mainstay of the economy of Mallaig for more than a century. Since Mallaig is the largest local village, this has an effect on the whole surrounding area. Fishing maintains jobs ashore, both through the associated industries of boat-maintenance, ice-making, porterage, transport, processing etc. and also because the families who are so maintained, live and spend their money locally. The West Highland fishing industry deserves a book to itself, and I shall do no more than point out some critical aspects:

a) Fishing continues to be of the first importance as a direct and indirect employer.

b) It involves government, both local and national, in helping provide the strategic infrastructure of roads and harbours. Government is also involved in issues of fishery policy: licences, quotas, international agreements, market support mechanisms and conservation measures.

c) It has good years and bad years. Fishing has always been cyclical in nature, and since such events were first recorded, there are plenty of examples of the success or failure of one or other species.

d) Many different species have been or are being fished for. These include pelagic fish (herring, mackerel, sprats), demersal fish (cod, haddock, whiting) and shellfish (lobsters, prawns, clams). Each of these has its own catching history.

e) One problem facing the industry is overfishing. Fishermen compete with each other not just in the sense that they pursue the same quarry but because their catching methods may be incompatible. Some techniques are better at conserving stocks than others. Trawlers and creel-boats have different interests. There is tension between fishermen from different areas about access rights and what catching methods are legitimate. There are political tensions arising from quotas based on what scientists see as desirable and what politicians view as acceptable.

f) Pollution. The marketing of shellfish has faced restrictions in recent years because of fears about toxicity. There is considerable debate about the causes of this, the sufferings of salmon and sea trout, and the various mishaps experienced by fish farmers. Blame is attributed to 'pollution' in a variety of forms. Allegations are often unspecific but there is undoubted unease about some of the methods used by fish farms.

The development of Mallaig was brought about by the conjunction of fishing and the railway. There had been an industry there for 50 years when the railway arrived at the very beginning of the twentieth century. But what the railway brought was access to the markets. Fish could now be taken to the great cities within a matter of hours, and early accounts of Mallaig give the impression of a boom town in the Wild West. There was tremendous bustle and economic activity, a Chinatown of sheds and kippering yards. The processing has largely gone but the village is still primarily a fishing village. It has its own fleet and serves as a port for a number of visiting boats.

Mallaig's boom times are associated with the pelagic fishery, in particular for herring. The west-coast sea-lochs were, for centuries, visited by immense shoals of herring from which the Highlanders did not benefit as much as they should have done. The days of great hauls of herring and dozens of kippering sheds may be over but there is always likely to be a market for quality fresh fish. The demand for shellfish may even increase with growing prosperity here and other European countries. It seems likely that there will continue to be a fishing fleet, and that it will remain a mainstay of the local economy, but that, with increasing catching power, it will employ fewer people.

It is also uncertain what sort of fishing industry it will be. The whole trend these days is towards sustainable methods of fishing. The creel-men may have the tide of public opinion on their side but traditional fishing communities, and their politicians, are not going to welcome restrictions they see as financially crippling. There is nothing new in this. Fishing has always been riven with controversy by the introduction of new catching methods.

Transport

The road and the railway run from Fort William to Mallaig. They are absolutely fundamental to the economic well-being of the area. We only have to look at the pattern of settlement and the changes to population distribution over the last two hundred years to confirm this. The price of survival is, in most cases, proximity to a road.

In the first half of the twentieth century the railway line had a higher relative importance. The railway employed a large number of people and carried quantities of commercial traffic. Fish trains ran right down the pier, shoals of herring steamed away to markets in the south, the tourists arrived by train. In the last few decades this has all changed. The fish trains have long since gone and the line now ends at the station. The shoals are now of tourists, many coming by train but many others by coach or car. Like the herring, they show cyclical variations.

Commercial traffic has largely deserted the railway; even heavy goods now come by lorry. This development, which is by no means unique to the West Highlands, has threatened the future of the railway line. On the one hand road freight offers more convenient distribution, on the other there are environmental concerns about the quantity of road traffic. There is also the issue of whether to maintain what is, for some, an essential social service. The long-term survival of the West Highland line depends on government strategy. Trains are busy in the summer, and the success of the steam train revival has provided a welcome fillip. Unfortunately there are still too few passengers for much of the winter.

There are certain advantages to be derived from Mallaig's geographical position as a critical node within the transport network. It is the railway terminus and also the ferry terminal for Skye and the Small Isles. These functions give some employment and a transport infrastructure. With people increasingly having the leisure and money to travel, this offers potential for the future. There are also opportunities for private enterprise. Local firms operate ferries to Knoydart from Mallaig and to the Small Isles from Arisaig.

There is potential for growth in the prosperous world of yachting and boating. Yachts need to be moored, provisioned and maintained. On the west coast of Argyll there are already several centres which offer winter storage and maintenance facilities. This industry has a presence in Arisaig, but not yet in Mallaig which would have to learn to accommodate the differing interests of fishermen and yachtsmen.

Tourism

Arisaig and Mallaig are destinations because they are ferry terminals for Skye and the Small Isles. Some local communities are tourist destinations in their own right. People have come for angling holidays in the area for nigh on two hundred years. The coastline between Arisaig and Morar has a summer influx of people on camping and caravanning holidays. But holiday patterns are changing and cheap air travel means that what would have been unthinkable in the past is now commonplace. Arisaig and Morar have to compete with other tourist resorts with better weather and fewer or no troublesome insects. More and better facilities are needed to persuade clients that holidays in the Highlands are still worth taking.

The tourist industry demands compromises from any local culture. These are not always made happily. There is a residual reluctance to put the needs of the tourist first. Nevertheless tourism plays a critical role in the Highland economy and is not always accorded the importance it deserves. Facilities such as the golf course at Traigh, the swimming pool, the visitor and heritage centres in Arisaig and Mallaig, are crucial in giving visitors a range of options for their holidays.

Society and Culture

The twentieth century has seen the cultural transformation of the area. The arrival of the railway line, the growth of Mallaig as a fishing port, the influx of families from other parts of Scotland and Britain: all have served to promote a demographic revolution in Mallaig and, to a certain extent, in Morar and Arisaig. This immigration has been going on for a long time and has never been regarded as an unmixed blessing. It used to be said of Morar that there were no sermons before the railway, meaning that the whole area was completely Catholic prior to this. Equally a quote from the Napier Commission allows us to view the delightfully ambiguous attitude of the Highlander towards the Sassenach incomer. Mr Mackenzie, factor for the Arisaig estate, regarded the under-factor, Mr Joseph Routledge, as a native, since he had been born and bred in the district and spoke Gaelic:

Q. I am afraid it is not a Highland name?
A. *That is his misfortune ... I wish he had.*

In the context of the debate about the decline of Gaelic it is significant that when the Routledges came to Arisaig they were themselves absorbed. The father of Mr Joseph Routledge was not a Highlander, but young Joseph was. However, whilst Arisaig society could absorb an innkeeper, the threat from another direction was more insidious. Mr Mackenzie was also a member of the School Board, although more than a little hazy on matters educational. Apparently there were three board Schools in the Inverness-shire portion of Ardnamurchan parish. He thought that none of the three teachers was Gaelic-speaking.

But the fact of the matter is that no Highland community has the luxury of standing still. Adapt or die – and all too many have died. One of the prices of economic change is a changed society and culture. This has happened in its own way in all three villages. It has not been without the occasional tension, but all in all it is quite extraordinary how such an amorphous body has been so successful. When looked at against other Highland communities, many of which have been marginalised or bled dry, this district has been strikingly resilient. There are areas of concern. Morar has recently lost its shop and post office. Fortunately its proximity to Mallaig protects it from terminal decline but it would certainly be preferable to have greater economic independence.

Language

In 1822 the Inverness Society for the Education of the Poor in the Highlands started an investigation into the state of education in the area. Unfortunately neither of the parishes covering our districts (Ardnamurchan for Arisaig and South Morar, Glenelg for North Morar) returned their schedules, but we have sufficient evidence from neighbouring areas to draw a likeness. The Synod of Glenelg included the presbyteries of Abertarff, Lochcarron, Skye, Uist and Lewis. (Lochcarron included the parish of Glenelg.) Out of 12,486 families, over 96% understood Gaelic best, less than 4% understood English best. The nearest mainland Argyllshire parish to send in returns was Ardchattan. Even here over 90% of the families understood Gaelic best.

Let us compare these results with those for the census returns in 1891 when the speaking of Gaelic was officially recorded. Despite a certain carelessness with regard to the language skills of tiny infants, over 96% of the population of North Morar spoke Gaelic, although an increasing number of these now spoke English as well.

Why is it that Gaelic has all but disappeared from the area? Lots of culprits have been identified – the Statutes of Iona in 1609, the use of English in official documents, the anglicisation of the clan chiefs, the Scottish education system, the influx of incomers in the twentieth century. Some of these can swiftly be laid to rest. The data from the census returns makes it clear that the overwhelming majority of locals still spoke Gaelic at the end of the nineteenth century. In fact, in 1836 Rev Alexander Beith supplies negative evidence from the parish of Glenelg:

Here, as throughout the whole Highlands, there exists the greatest ambition for the acquirement of English. Without it, it is well known there is little probability of advancing in the world; but from the system pursued in our schools, the progress hitherto made in introducing English has been limited indeed.

There are perhaps two factors that are more important than any others. The first is that universal free education was instituted in the last quarter of the nineteenth century – in English. The second is that economic and social changes brought Arisaig and Morar into greater contact with the rest of Britain. James Macdonald, a local man, reflected on the effects of such commerce:

The railway has, however, completely changed the good old chivalrous element, into a most insipid and uninteresting one, and the old gaelic tongue, I notice, begins to wince visibly at the corrosions which that saucy English language tries to make.

Another theory as to why Gaelic has largely disappeared in Arisaig is not the flood of adult immigrants, but the flood of children. In the twentieth century Arisaig provided a home for significant numbers of 'boarded-out' children. The argument goes that the language of the playground became English rather than Gaelic.

Now the wheel has come full circle with the promotion of Gaelic-medium education. The new position is one of official as well as popular sympathy for a minority language. This is long overdue, but perhaps not sufficient to re-establish it. Since the late nineteenth century nothing has proved so inimical to Gaelic as the Scottish educational system.

Material Culture

The twentieth century saw erratic but continued progress in standards of material culture, health care and education. The infrastructure is all in place. There is electricity and a phone system, a six-year secondary school, three primary schools, doctors, a visiting dentist, a health clinic etc. The standard of living and level of social service available in the rest of Britain have been slowly extended into the Highlands. These threaten a traditional Highland way of life but we cannot argue with people who want to watch television rather than hear folklore, who listen to pop music rather than learn Gaelic songs, who play with their computers rather than make a creel or milk a cow. Such preferences are impossible to dispute. We can bewail such choices, mourn the death of a traditional culture, but if people vote against it with their lifestyles, then nostalgia is misplaced.

Where are we going?

When it comes to foretelling the future, the historian's opinion is worth no more than anyone else's, so I will confine myself to the transmission of history and heritage.

In material terms there is little built heritage to transmit. Few houses are old, and since most of these are in private hands they will last or not as their owners choose. Much local history is locked into the landscape where, in the absence of development, it is relatively safe. The sculpture in Kilmory is in urgent need of preservation, and old place-names should be written down before they are lost for ever.

The last native Gaelic speakers will come under increasing pressure and new ones will learn the language for leisure or interest. Children will be tied to global cultural trends. They will know more about American or Australian soaps than what happened in their own locality in the past. Is this important? Does it matter? Yes! The Highlands had distinctive systems of social organisation and land-tenure. They enjoyed a distinct military, political and cultural history. If all memory and understanding of this is discarded, then something defining is lost.

There is a grievous presumption that Highland history is not worthwhile. It features little in the Scottish educational curriculum. It is ironic that the tourist industry probably does more to promote Highland history than all the universities and schools put together. The history of the Highlands is more than the Jacobites and the Clearances. It is more than romance and tragedy; it is also about economics, the struggle with the environment, and cultural and artistic aspiration. It is in this spirit that I offer this as *a* history, rather than *the* history, of Arisaig and Morar.

EPILOGUE

How we see the past is crucial to our vision of the future. To be nostalgic is part of the human condition, but there is self-deception when we gaze back through rose-tinted spectacles. If we mistake a wasteland for a wilderness, a state of decay for a state of nature, then we do ourselves and our history a disservice. In the same way that a lot of romantic pap is written about people in the past, so there is a great deal of gushing prose about the landscape.

The Highlands were a *peopled* landscape. Population levels have fluctuated, and certainly some of the hinterland may always have been an unkind waste of trees and wolves, but the coastline has been settled ever since Man returned to Scotland after the last Ice Age. To presuppose that this area was formerly natural or wild leads to restrictive practice by planners and bureaucrats. There are strong pressures against development in a 'natural' environment. It must not be 'spoiled'. Roads should not be built, drains dug or cables laid. Houses, schools, factories should not be constructed except in designated places.

There are sometimes good reasons for this central direction. Some regulations work for the common good. Local authorities do not want to take on commitments to provide services in new and expensive locations. Against this it must be recognised that to deny economic opportunities in areas as fragile as the West Highlands merely aggravates the economic condition. Bureaucratic regulation can help keep the Highlands the desert they have become. Better still if developments can be denied under the guise of 'conservation'. The Highlands are subsidised by Edinburgh, and Edinburgh decides what economic developments are environmentally acceptable. He who pays the piper ...

There is an unconscious acceptance of the present Highland scene as 'natural'. In many, perhaps most, areas it is not. It is a *damaged* landscape, a man-made desert created by two centuries of unrestricted grazing by sheep and deer. The question of what the Highlands were once like is keenly debated, but in Arisaig and Morar it is safe to say that the former scene contained more natural woodland, much more managed grassland and many patches of cultivation. There were lots of cattle, horses and goats, relatively few sheep or deer. By 1838 the minister for Ardnamurchan parish was noticing physical changes as a result of the expansion of sheep-walks. He gave warning of 'extensive tracts of outfield arable relapsing into their original barrenness, in consequence of being included in these pastures'.

Today, the issue of whether or not the climate is changing is the subject of keen debate. This is not new. In 1894 Aeneas Macdonell of Camusdarroch gave anecdotal evidence about climate change and deterioration in the quality of pasture. By spade husbandry he meant use of the *cas-chrom* or foot-plough:

> I may also state as a general fact ... that the pasturage is very much deteriorated compared with what it used to be. It certainly is in that portion of Arisaig to which I refer, in my own observation. Of course, I believe that the climate has very much changed and affected the pasture; but more, much more, has the want of cropping done so. The spade husbandry, which was then in vogue, was employed so that every inch of cultivable ground at that time was manured and put into good heart. Even now it is apparent that the land that is cultivated by the crofters in every place has better pasture and is improved by them so that it is superior to what is under either sheep or deer. At the same time even the crofters' pasture is not so good as it was, in consequence of the wetter weather that prevails as compared with what there was in my young days. We used to have deep snow that lay for weeks, perhaps even months, when roads were impassable to any vehicle; but when the sun melted away, the grass sprouted up in abundance, and there was plenty for all the cattle to consume during the winter.

Deer Forest Commission, Arisaig, 1894

Youth is ever gilded and it will probably never be possible to offer more than anecdotal support for Aeneas Macdonell's opinions. However, in *The Roads from the Isles,* D Pochin Mould gives the following quotation about Hanoverian patrols in the years after Culloden:

Lieut. Maxwell from Tray, in Morarr, informs me, he has made several attempts since last Report to send out Patroles, but they were prevented by the Snow and wth much difficulty returned to Quarters. He adds, that he is assured that it will not be in his Power to patrole any more this season.

    5 November 1750, report from the Loch Arkaig station

On the other hand, between 1834 and 1838 Colonel Robertson Macdonald of Kinlochmoidart kept meteorological records which appeared in the New Statistical Account. The coldest monthly mean temperature was 32 in February 1838. Winter monthly means in the upper 30s and above were the norm. As Rev M'Lean said:

The climate is undoubtedly temperate, though exceedingly variable. Snow, which scarcely ever falls heavily, seldom lasts longer than twenty-four hours on the low grounds, though on the higher hills it may continue for months.

Truth, about the weather, is always difficult to establish!

The dependence on road transport and the failure to maintain a maritime communications network compounds the economic problems of the Highlands. To be beside a road is now a precondition for economic survival. Not many of the old settlements could satisfy this, and so they have withered and died. To be accessible by boat is irrelevant today. Yet in previous centuries almost every community in the West Highlands and Hebrides met this condition.

Inaction compounds decay. One of the biggest problems about private ownership of land is the lack of power in the hands of the community. There is a sense of being helpless and ineffectual. This will never be solved by crofting ownership of the land, although it might by public ownership. Private ownership, however beneficent, has meant that all economic decisions in the Highlands are taken by tiny but powerful minorities. Today, increasingly, the land is in the hands of quangos and wildlife organisations. There is justifiable doubt that these new elites will prove any more sympathetic or accountable than the old.

To do nothing compounds decay in the landscape, and confirms decay in the cultural heritage. Every carved stone lying exposed in every churchyard in the West Highlands is subject to assault by the elements. Sometimes, as in Arisaig, stones that were not originally supposed to be graveslabs have been borrowed as such. In the last

80 years Arisaig's single mediaeval carving of Christ has disintegrated or disappeared. It is doubly unfortunate that this has occurred in, of all places, a churchyard. It would be pleasing to preserve what remains before it is too late.

A knowledge of history enriches our present perspective. It does not make us any poorer if we appreciate the complexities of the past. We may have to give up some of our simplistic views about the Clearances and Bonnie Prince Charlie, but this does not make Highland history less valuable. On the contrary, when we see how people faced the same moral dilemmas as us, when we understand the complexities of their economic and political choices, it makes the past more, not less, intriguing.

SELECT BIBLIOGRAPHY

This is not an exhaustive bibliography. It is intended as a guide to further reading for those who become sufficiently interested to pursue their own research.

Letters to and from David Bruce, and his report, are found in Vol. 99 of the Hardwicke Papers, British Library.

The sources for the Arisaig and Morar rentals are given in Figure 8. The list of Morar place-names referred to in Chapter 2 is from Father E. J. Macdonald's papers, Archives of Ontario.

Throughout this book I have followed the convention of referring to the 'Old' and 'New' Statistical Accounts. Technically the former was not 'old'.

Arisaig Scrapbook, Arisaig WRI

Boulton, Plan of North Morar, 1834 (National Archives of Scotland (RHP 3687))

British Geological Survey, Arisaig, 1″ : 1 mile (Solid Edition)

British Geological Survey, Arisaig, 1″ : 1 mile (Drift Edition)

Collectanea de Rebus Albanicis, Edinburgh, 1847

Deer Forest Commission, Edinburgh, 1895

Journall and Memoirs of P ... C ... Expedition into Scotland etc. by a Highland Officer in his Army, Lockhart Papers, Vol II, London, 1817

List of Persons Concerned in the Rebellion, Scottish History Society, Edinburgh, 1890

Muster Roll of Prince Charles Edward Stuart's Army, Aberdeen University Press, 1984

New Statistical Account, Vol VII (Parish of Ardnamurchan for Arisaig & South Morar), 1845

New Statistical Account, Vol XIV (Parish of Glenelg for North Morar), 1845

Old Statistical Account, Vol VIII (Parish of Ardnamurchan for Arisaig & South Morar), 1791–9

Old Statistical Account, Vol XVII (Parish of Glenelg for North Morar), EP Publishing, 1981

Prisoners of the '45, Sir Bruce Gordon Seton, Scottish History Society, Edinburgh, 1928

Report of the Napier Commission, Vol III, Edinburgh, 1884

R Black, *Mac Mhaighstir Alasdair – The Ardnamurchan Years*, Society of West Highland & Island Historical Research, 1986

O Blundell, *Catholic Highlands of Scotland* (Western Highlands and Islands), 1917

O Blundell, 'Notes on the church ... in Arisaig, etc.', in *Proceedings of the Society of Antiquaries of Scotland*, Vol 45, 1911

L A Boiteux, 'Un Baroud d'Honneur: Le Mars et la Bellone en Ecosse', *Revue d'histoire diplomatique*, 1959

H Cheape, 'Woodlands on the Clanranald Estates', in *Scotland since Prehistory*, ed. T C Smout, Scottish Cultural Press, Aberdeen, 1993

D Christison, *Early Fortifications in Scotland*, Edinburgh, 1898

M E M Donaldson, *Wanderings in the Western Highlands and Islands*, Paisley, 1923

Rev R Forbes, *The Lyon in Mourning*, Scottish History Society, 1895–7

C Fraser-Mackintosh, *Antiquarian Notes*, Inverness, 1897

P Galbraith, *Blessed Morar*, 1989

J Hogg, *Highland Tours*, Hawick, 1981

W Jolly, 'Cupped stones near Arisaig', *Proceedings of the Society of Antiquaries of Scotland*, 1882

J Knox, *A Tour through the Highlands of Scotland ... in 1786*, London, 1787

A D Lacaille, *The Stone Age in Scotland*, Oxford University Press, 1954

A Lang ed., *The Highlands of Scotland in 1750*, London, 1898

H Lumsden, 'Notice of some fragments ... in ... Arasaig', *Proceedings of the Society of Antiquaries of Scotland*, 1884

J Macculloch, *The Highlands and Western Isles of Scotland*, London, 1824

A and A Macdonald, *The Poems of Alexander Macdonald*, Inverness, 1924

James Macdonald, *Tales of the Highlands*, Inverness, 1907

Rev C Macdonald, *Moidart; or among the Clanranalds*, Oban, 1889

I R Mackay, 'Glenalladale's Settlement, Prince Edward Island', *Scottish Gaelic Studies*, 1963

R Munro, *Ancient Scottish Lake-Dwellings or Crannogs*, Edinburgh, 1882

R W Munro, *Taming the Rough Bounds*, Society of West Highland and Island Historical Research, 1984

D Rixson, *North Morar (1750–1900)*, Mallaig Heritage Centre, 1997

D Rixson, *Arisaig and South Morar*, Mallaig Heritage Centre, 1997

D Rixson, *Knoydart (1750–1894)*, Mallaig Heritage Centre, 1995

D and M Rixson, *The Rough Bounds*, Fort William, 1982

R Somers, *Letters from the Highlands*, Inverness, 1977

W Wood, *Moidart and Morar*, Edinburgh, 1950

INDEX